Jesse Foot

A Defence of the Planters in the West-Indies

Comprised in four arguments

Jesse Foot

A Defence of the Planters in the West-Indies
Comprised in four arguments

ISBN/EAN: 9783337318697

Printed in Europe, USA, Canada, Australia, Japan

Cover: Foto ©ninafisch / pixelio.de

More available books at **www.hansebooks.com**

A

DEFENCE

OF THE

PLANTERS in the WEST-INDIES;

COMPRISED IN FOUR ARGUMENTS

I. On Comparative Humanity,
II. On Comparative Slavery,
III. On the African Slave Trade,

AND

IV. On the Condition of Negroes in the Weft-Indies.

———————

By JESSÉ FOOT, Surgeon.

———————

NOMO SUM: HUMANI NIHIL A ME ALIENUM PUTO.

Terent. Heut.

I AM A MAN AND FEEL FOR ALL MANKIND.

Coleman.

———————

THE SECOND EDITION.

———————

LONDON:

PRINTED FOR J. DEBRETT, OPPOSITE BURLINGTON-HOUSE, PICCADILLY.

1792.

I HAVE no apology to offer for having gone out of the line of my profeffion in addreffing thefe arguments to the publick, no more than I fhould for having affifted in extinguifhing a fire that was burning down a houfe or a temple of worfhip. When the paffions are ftorming reafon, it is the duty of every focial man to endeavour at leaft to ftop their ravages—*Quod omnes tangit, ab omnibus tractari debet.*

I afpire to the hope of convincing rational men only—I leave the palm of fpiritualifing ideotifm to modern pioneers in humanity—to thofe who falfely begin at the bottom and dig up to the furface.

I fhould be happy to congratulate the planters that after the 2d of April they would be fafely landed on fhore, when future affiftance would be only an incumbrance ; but I do not flatter my opinion with a belief, that when this fubject meets with a fecond overthrow on that day, Enthufiafm will then let it fleep in peace. —The brains may be out, but the man will not die.—The planters are ftill to be toffed about in the turbulent ocean of prejudice ; their reputations are ftill to be expofed to waves after waves— mountain high—breaking their force upon them. Such will be the refult as long as paffion triumphs over truth.

The city of London have at length come to the point ; and after five years deliberation, have decided, on the 21ft of this month, againft petitioning for the abolition

of

of the flave-trade. They have weighed the whole of the queftion, and have not been feduced into a decifion by a partial and infidious reprefentation. Let this be an example—let others remember that they cannot decide juftly without being poffeffed of the whole of the truth in every caufe that comes before them.

We appear aftonifhed when we fee the multitude led away by founds : but we fhould remember that if founds work miracles it is always upon ignorance. The influence of names is in exact proportion to the want of knowledge.

J. F.

DEAN-STREET, SOHO,
MARCH 25, 1792.

A

DEFENCE of the PLANTERS

IN THE

WEST-INDIES.

On Comparative Humanity.

IT may feem, that he, who now takes up the pen to convey his fentiments upon Negroe-Slavery, appears at a late hour and after the fubject has been amply difcuffed; that he comes like a gleaner into the field, when the crop of grain is carried in, and can only add by handfuls to the common ftock.

A fpectator who has watched, with fome attention, the combatants upon this fubject, and who has feen the conteft between them eagerly conducted with more of paffion than reafon, may be confidered as ripening his judgment during their heat of altercation, and as correcting his own by their mifapprehenfions.

One is vexed to fee declaimers upon humanity abufing and degrading that noble paffion. Men ought firft of all to fhew to the world, that they know well how to define *what is humanity*,

B   before

before they begin to make a diftribution of it, to convince the world—that their reafon is awake to the purpofes of it—that they poffefs the actual paffion, and not its counterfeit—and that when they do beftow it, it is done under the difcretion of reafon.

I fhall firft of all define what humanity is, and then appropriate a diftribution of it as it ought for comforting active induftry and paffive exift-ence.

Humanity is a paffion infufed into our firft nature: it is a native ingredient in the compo-fition of man: it is *one of many more* focial vir-tues: it is that paffion which reafon preferves with the ftricteft caution, and diftributes with the exacteft juftice—that paffion which fhould not be lavifhed indifcriminately, and which is leaft likely to be fo when beft underftood.

How a man in a ftate of nature would difpofe of his humanity, it is naturally to be conceived. He would apply this focial paffion in a direction to his own happinefs—for obtaining additional comfort in his family, for enlarging his relative happinefs with his neighbour, for procuring good will to the right and the left of his own threfhold, and for making his own home a trea-fure of felicity, fecured from annoyance, becaufe it was protected by innocence.

This would be the full extent of humanity in a ftate of nature.

But

But in that ftate which is called civilifation, whether properly or not I will not now fay, humanity is to be confidered in many various ways.

Where fome poffefs abundant wealth, and others are moft miferably poor—where fome muft dig that ore which brightens in the purfes of others—where fome muft cultivate that foil for others who take away the produce—where fome muft weave the cloth for others to wear upon their backs—where fome muft be common fol-diers, and act under the direction of the paffions of others—and where fome muft be failors, and muft fubmit to be torn from their families, to be dragged like criminals away from their homes, and perhaps never again to be reftored—Whilft thefe are *neceffary* gradations in a *civilifed fociety,* and whilft it is found *neceffary* that thefe various gradations in the conditions of men fhall exift, fo long will it be *neceffary* for that fociety to con-fider how to apply its humanity—not with a *partial hand,* nor with an *unnatural impulfe,* but with a general view to the conditions of the whole.

If I, therefore, fpoke of a private man, he will, if he obeys the impulfe of nature, com-mence his career of humanity with his relatives and his neighbours—if I fpoke of the public, they ought, when they commence their career of humanity, to beftow it with an even hand, to pour it through every channel where the cries of it moft *immediately, directly,* and *loudly* affail their ears and hearts.

Under

Under the prefent circumftances of this country, no one will be fo bold as to fay that we can
difpenfe with the induftry of the miner, the collier, the ploughman, and the weaver, or with the
poft of the foldier or failor. To have it in our
power to meliorate their conditions, preferve
their health, and by ftrict attention exemplarily
habituate them to fobriety and induftry, is
one thing—to have for ever neglected it, is another.

All that humanity can do, for foftening the
hard conditions of thofe in active fociety, is to
reward induftry and correct licentioufnefs—to
block up every avenue that leads to depravity—
to put it out of the power of a labourer to con-
fume his time when he is able to employ it—
and to allow no temptation for a wafte of the
wages of induftry in the finks of intoxication.

The effects of intoxication, and more efpecially by fpirituous liquors, tend to enervate the
frame, ftarve the family, depreciate its children,
lead on the taker to the perpetration of horrid
crimes, and caft him at length into a *folitary*
dungeon.

If I faw the publick career of humanity com-
mencing with thefe confiderations, I fhould be
affured that as it refers to active fociety, the purpofe was unqueftionable, and that the paffion
which moved the judgment was not only fincere
but juft.

But

But when 1 fee thefe conditions of men neglected—conditions which muft be feen, but dif-
regarded—which obtrude upon ourfenfesat home
and abroad—in all our paths, at our own doors,
in the open ftreets, and in all the public roads—
when I fee a new dungeon erecting in every
county, and the art of mafonry ftrained for the
inclufion of human wretchednefs—when I fee
dram-fhops increafing becaufe the revenue is
increafed by it—when I fee the very thief-
takers applying *there* to feize their deluded victims—when I fee the keepers of thofe fhops
diftributing the poifon withouta pang, and gree-
dily griping the mifapplied fractions of induftry
to pay the revenue office—when I fee that thefe
practices pafs uncorrected, and that the country
is reduced to the neceffity of raifing a revenue
for the fupport of its credit by thefe defperate
means—I look with indignity on that falfe humanity which leads men in fearch after the con-
'dition of negroes, far beyond the reach of their
eyes and the genuine impulfes of their hearts,
whilft fuch ftriking temptations for the practice
of the pofitive paffion obtrude upon their reafon
on every fide they turn.

Is it not more humane to prevent crimes than
to punifh them ? and is there a man who reflects,
and who does not know that immorality, ex-
treme poverty, and the moft defperate acts, are
promoted by, if not founded upon, an eafy accefs

to

to fpirituous liquors? Who does not know that the way is made eafy in defiance of humanity, merely to increafe the revenue? Who does not know that the very fyftem is founded in inhumanity? that it rends the focial bands into pieces? totally counteracts the operations of morality? and that the Chriftian religion lofes all its influence over a mind deadened to every virtuous impreffion, difeafed beyond reformation;—that it is in the eftablifhment of no effect, and that the occupation is a mere dead letter?

The miftake of the prefent age is, that men enquire into the effects of crimes, and neglect the caufes.

There can be but two caufes affigned for the miferable condition of the loweft clafs of people in this country; either there is not work enough for them, or they mifapply the earnings of their labour. Moft of their mifery is derived from their licentioufnefs, and no attempts are made by the legiflature for the prevention of it.

Nor has the attention of private characters, who have embarked in the noble caufe of humanity, been engaged to the *prevention* of crimes:—*not* to point out the means whereby thofe devoted victims which are found in prifons *may be prevented from coming to that end*—*not* to turn them from the path that leads to the folitary cell—but *how* they are *to be accommodated on their arrival there.*

Had

Had Mr. Howard confined his enquiry to that which is within the ability of one private man, and had his paffion of humanity been regulated by the controul of reafon, and not by enthufiafm amounting to Quixotifm, he might have traced the progrefs of depravity from the bud, and have been enabled to point out thofe means of prevention which are more effential acts of humanity than the univerfal fludy of prifons.

What are the conditions of other focieties to us, if that fociety we live in be fo wretched and depraved, as to call loudly for our direct attention? Are we not compelled by the force of reafon to correct the defperate conditions of thofe in our own *ftate*, and *before our own nofes*, before we are authorifed in confcience to examine farther off?—to clear our own prifons—to thin our own workhoufes—to clothe our own beggars—to fee that our own induftrious fhall not perifh from want or licentioufnefs, and to watch with a fteady eye their firft attempts to depravity?—to check the growing evil—to lock up the doors of dram-fhops—to diftinguifh the induftrious from the idle—to follow up difcarded fervants and difbanded foldiers and failors—to enquire into the caufe of empty churches?

Afcertaining the characters of the fufpicious—providing employ for thofe who will work—

com-

compelling thofe who otherwife would not—and
punifhing quickly thofe who have offended—is
of more importance, in the fcale of humanity,
than all the plans of jails in England, and
fchemes againft flavery in the W. Indies, that
enthufiafm for one or the other ever fuggefted.

Humanity diftributed by an enthufiaft will
ever be mifapplied. Reafon muft have a controul over the paffion of humanity. The mind
muft be firm and the conftitution found. There
muft be *mens fana in corpore fano.* He who dif-
pofes of his humanity under the influence of
dotage or ftrong affection will pervert the paffion, becaufe it was not regulated by judgment.
If it be thus difpofed by will, to be diftributed
after death, as it very frequently is towards publick endowments, relatives then fuffer by the
mifapplication. The cafe of the late Mr. Ruf-
fell, who, under this difeafed influence, left his
all to endowments, and his kindred to ftarve,
will exemplify what I mean. And if it be thus
difpofed in the lifetime of the giver, he will
fuffer by the mifapplication. It is very immaterial to my argument, whether the ftory be
real or fancied; but the immortal bard has
brought the fate of King Lear, who gave his
all, fo home to our bofoms—has fo realifed the
mifapplication of humanity—that it would be
dotage indeed not to feel how directly it is
within the pale of nature.

An

An *Enthufiaft* becomes fo heated in the purfuit of his object, as to exceed the limitation of
common reafon and plain underftanding. *Humanity* ftands in need of no fuch *hot-bed*. It is
found to be of the moft pofitive nature in a man
with a cool head and common generofity—in his
greateft vigour of mind—in the prime of his life—
and when he holds an intercourfe with fociety.

It is only a part of the character of a good
man.—It is that part which he can ftill be beftowing and ftill retain enough—It is that fountain from the heart which can -never be ex-
haufted—It is that which, when diffufed, creates
a reverence for the giver, and *excites an example
which others can follow*—It is a difcharge of duty
as a focial being, in a difcreet manner. Whereas
by adopting this paffion in exclufion of all others
—by applying it to one object, and neglecting
every other—by exceeding that which is beyond
the reach or ability of the reft in fociety, the end
cannot be obtained, becaufe *one alone* is not adequate to it, and the chafe is given up becaufe
more cannot follow the Enthufiaft in it.

It muft be remembered that the enquiry of
Mr. Howard into the ftate of prifons, and the
inquiry of Mr. Wilberforce into the ftate of
negroe flaves, were both of them topicks agitated at one and the fame time. Whilft Mr.
Howard was laying down the plan for immuring
prifoners in *folitary dungeons* in order to *reform*

C   *them,*

them, Mr. Wilberforce was knocking off the imaginary chains from the negroes in the West Indies—counting the lashes of the cart-whip upon their backs—and taking them out of the stocks, which is their only place of confinement, in order to *reform their severe task-masters.*

I have watched these proceedings which have attracted popularity, and have smiled with contempt at the absurdity of them.

Why had not Mr. Wilberforce, whilst Mr. Howard was contriving new accommodations for prisoners—whilst every county was employing architects for new plans and new elevations of prison-houses—moved in the House of Commons for an enquiry into the causes which produced so dreadful a necessity ? Why have not the obsequious chartered boroughs, and the manufacturing towns, charged their Members with petitions upon these causes as well as that upon the Slave Trade ? Have they omitted to do so because they knew of those evils which existed in the *West Indies,* but were ignorant of any existing in *England ?*

I do not mean to appeal to the passions, but to the common sense of my countrymen ; and I do say, that neither the dungeon, Botany Bay, or the gallows, will avail any thing in reforming the corrupted morals of the age. The time (as some say) is now come when money is profusely plenty—when taxes are to be taken off—and when the publick funds are as high as they were ever
known

known to have been. Is not this a fitting time then for providing individual comforts—for checking immorality—for inculcating fobriety and induftry—and for making the loweft clafs of people virtuoufly happy?

Human nature is a flave to habit. Reformation can only advance by convincing the underftanding of the fuperior benefits which will be the refult of it : and the underftanding muft be in a ftate of fobriety for receiving the impreffion with any intention of effect. Prevention of drunkennefs is almoft the firft and the only neceffary ftep. The fever excited upon the brain by inebriety muft firft fubfide, before reafon will be liftened to ; and yet (notwithftanding we are faid to be in a flourifhing ftate), we are to be told that the revenue would fuffer, if the ufe of fpirituous liquors were forbidden.

The morality of the lower clafs of people is their beft fecurity for order and decency. Whoever tempts them on that point, whether it be an individual or any collective body of men, either as legiflators or any other, are as highly criminal as thofe they thus vitiate.

Methinks it would be a curious predicament to view the Commons of England in—if that—whilft the Minifter is haranguing on the profperous ftate of the finances, and whilft the Surplus of the Revenue is dwelt upon with more than ordinary triumph—they fhould be fo hardy in the fame

breath

breath to fay that the revenue drawn from the
fale of fpirits was now pofitively neceffary for the
fupport of the ftate—and that at leaft two thoufand houfes in the metropolis fhould be neceffarily
kept open for dealing out indifcriminately the
poifon to men, women, and children. Who
can reflect upon this without horror, knowing at
the fame time, as we do, that the practice is
encouraged becaufe of the fupport it yields to
the ftate ? If this be not the proftitution of morality and humanity brought home to our hearts,
I cannot fee it in *Africa*, in *Afia*, or in *America*:
there is no fuch temptation—it is all a vifion—
there is no neceffity for a *reform any where*.

Is fuch the practice of humanity, which is to
be diffufed by example ? To expect reforms
from thofe provided for in office, I know is to
look for a thing where it cannot be found. But
I wonder how the nation at large can behold in
filence, and without emotions that proclaim their
aftonifhment, the erections of larger jails—the
beggars in the ftreets—the open debaucheries—
the loofe language of drunkards affailing the ears
of virtue—the fwarms of wretches configned to
workhoufes, or pining in want, fecluded in garrets
—and moreover than all this, the increafe of
parochial taxes year after year. Such things
are : and yet we are to be told that we are con-
fcientioufly in a ftate for enquiring into the mifery of thofe under the care and protection of
others.

If

If Mr. Burke fays that the *age of chivalry* is gone, I fay that the *age of humanity* is gone. To relieve the wants of our fellow citizens is a duty of government; the conftitution by which it is upheld has commanded it : to extend humanity beyond that which duty has prefcribed *is optional.*

If the combined talents of eminent men had been employed in inveftigating the condition of human mifery at home which prevails at this time, and had given vigour in checking the immoralities of the loweft clafs of people by the force of their examples, emanations of humanity would have then been juftly excited and naturally diffufed, becaufe the impulfe would have accorded with reafon. The fpirit of enquiry would have gone forth—vice would be checked before it be too far gone—and the induftrious in diftrefs would be familiarly diftinguifhed from the idle and abandoned : but the workhoufe, that common fink, receives all without diftinction, except thofe who are imprifoned or configned to a fate beyond redemption.

Inftead of fuch inveftigations which preffed hard upon us as a duty, we have all along been diverted from them by remoter topicks—by the abolition of the flave-trade—and the flavery of Frenchmen.

Our very publick hofpitals, in this age of affected humanity, would have been bankrupted,

and

and the wards fhut up, if the contributions had not been increafed by mufical meetings. It was not the voluntary tribute of charity, arifing from the impulfe of the heart *immediately* ; it was not the hand of humanity that gave the boon *directly* ; but it was charmed from the purfe by the effect of mufick on the ears, by that fame paffage that brains are extracted in preparing Egyptian mummies.

St. George's and the Middlefex hofpitals were erected by voluntary contributions before the new buildings in Marybone were begun ; and notwithftanding the wonderful increafe there of the richeft inhabitants, not a wing has been added to either—for the contributions have failed !

The city charities flourifh. Honeft induftry, rewarded by opulence, invigorates the mind. Many *there* now in affluence, fprung from poor parents—they know where diftrefs pinches, and nature points out the remedy. London has not preffed on the Houfe of Commons for abolifhing the flave trade—London looks to the preffing objects of humanity nearer home—it petitioned for the abolition of the fhop-tax, and made its Members vote as they ought.

Taxes impofed beyond that point which can be borne, is the greateft flavery that can be inflicted. I appeal to every collector of taxes, whether he can imagine real diftrefs exifting in a greater degree, than that he fees

3   through-

throughout this metropolis ? Do not let us lay
the flattering unction to the breaft, and conclude
that all are content who do not murmur. Defpair has its fits, and when it can only rave in
vain it will rather mope in filence.

If I heard, that, now we are at peace, a confi-
deration of the prefent ftate of the fubjects who
are at a time of life for employments of active
induftry was to be directly gone into by Parliament—if I heard that it was their determination
to abolifh every tax which tended to encourage
fuch practices as depraved the human mind—if
I heard that the idle were obliged to work, and
that their wages could not be fpent in intoxication—if I heard that the conditions of the poor
were ferioufly confidered, and that immorality
and profanenefs no longer defiled our ftreets—
if I found that we had more humanity than
would effect thefe reforms at home—I would
vote for beftowing the furplus without hefitation
on any other fubjects in the world that claimed it
from their fufferings. But let us commence the
duties belonging to citizens of the world *after*
we have difcharged the more relative duties exacted from us to the poor of our own country. This
would be acting upon a warrantable fyftem, and
would leave no doubt upon the minds of men
that the motive fprung from *pofitive humanity.*

The Minifter, who fays that by the abolition
of fpirituous liquors fo much revenue would be
loft

loft to the ftate, has but little infight into the
operation of that poifon upon the conftitution.
It does not produce a fimilar intoxication to
malt liquors ; nor is the habit of drinking fpirits
confined to the feafon of focial enjoyment : it
excites the moft furious paffions—inflames the
brain—leads men on to riot—and often to the
perpetration of murder.

The act of *Captain Wilfon* is as worthy of re-
cord as the continence of a *Scipio* or the virtue
of a *Cato* ; who, when his fhip was loft on the
Pelew Iflands, induced his crew to ftave the
cafks of fpirituous liquors, left they fhould change
the ftate of preffing danger into irrevocable defpair, and quarrel with the natives, when they
knew not what they did.

The money which is confumed by this infa-
mous practice of drinking fpirits would be laid
out in comfortable commodities that are already
taxed; and although the revenue from fpirituous
liquors would be funk, that from other commodities would be increafed, more labour would be
applied to the welfare of the ftate, and the poor
rates would be fenfibly reduced. This is the
beft argument that can be offered, and it is that
which will find the readieft way to the heart of
a Minifter. Tell him that the revenue will not
fuffer, but be increafed ; and although he might
not yield to a reform from the motive of humanity,

manity, yet he will more likely from that of intereft.

I do affert that there is no condition, no gradation of men in this country, that may not be made comfortable and taken from the brink of defpair, provided the attention of thofe whofe duty it is, be engaged to it.

Every miferable object that prefents itfelf fhould have at leaft an hearing, and every diftrefs fhould be inveftigated; *then* it would be apparent whether thofe who fall—fall from inevitable misfortune or from vicious propenfities. This is that humanity which we are moft preffingly called upon to difcharge; and when we have done fo much, we may with clean hands and light hearts enquire into remoter conditions.

Have the Members of the Houfe of Commons, who liftened with fo much attention to the abolition of the flave-trade, and who have fhewed fuch a promptitude at declaiming upon the doubtful evidence of miferies unfeen, ripened their humanity for meliorating the pofitive fufferings of thofe objects evident to our fenfes? Have they reflected upon the comparative call for their humanity at home with that which Mr. Wilberforce exacts for Africans? or are they befotted by the *necromantick power of African magicians,* and cannot break the fpell?

Befides the application of humanity to thofe in a condition for active induftry at home, there

is an humanity due to thofe who are in a ftate *only*
of paffive exiftence—to thofe who have paffed
the age for labour, and to thofe who have not as
yet arrived to the age for labour.

No ftate can flourifh without population; and
I will take it upon myfelf to prove that there is
no ftate, in no part of the globe, where the care of
population is more neglected than in this country.
Medical affiftance and medical influence with
thofe in the habit of drinking fpirits is all out of
the queftion. I will appeal to medical men for
an anfwer to thefe facts—whether thoufands of
children do not perifh for want of care—whether the mothers who drink fpirits do not deftroy
their children who fuck them—whether thofe
who furvive be not pitiable objects—and whether many do not now fall a facrifice to the
fmall-pox which could be faved?

When Mr. Wilberforce again commences his
inquiries into the ftate of negroes upon the coaft
of Africa, along the middle paffage, and in the
Weft-Indies—when he is again moved by the
yearning of humanity—I invite him, as a relief
to thofe fcenes abroad, to turn his attention to
the comparative ftate of wretchednefs at home;
let him call before a Committee of the Houfe of
Commons fome of the miferable objects of this
country—let thefe fpeak for themfelves—let him
be but half as inquifitive in the inveftigation of
their conditions as he has been in that of the negroes,

groes, and then *go to his supper with what appetite he may.*

If Mr. Burke, who pleads with all the fire of Demofthenes for kingly rights, and who fupports the crown with an uplifted arm—if Mr. Payne, who urges the rights of man with the nervous mind of Lycurgus, and tramples the crown under his feet—if they had employed their pens on the fide of pofitive humanity, and had left kings to defend themfelves, by their own arguments—by the *ultima ratio regum*—by the thunder of their cannon—they would have both been feen in a nobler caufe.

If Mr. Fox and Mr. Burke had but employed half the force of their powers of oratory on this theme that they confumed on the ftate of Frenchmen, they would to this day have been mutual friends, and gone down to pofterity with the fame blefling from the wretched in England upon both.

As to Mr. Pitt—I have no hope in him. He who deftroyed fmuggling for the fake of the revenue alone, and radically encouraged fpirituous liquors by granting more favourable licences—he who could foment a conteft for Weftminfter, and fupport an unconftitutional fcrutiny for more than twelve months—he who could thus decifively promote inordinate tumults and intoxication—it would be vain to fearch for, in any corner of his heart, a fingle feed

of

of humanity. But if the ſpirit of humanity be not dead, but only ſlumbering—if it can be rouſed at the clamorous appeal of neceſſity, its cries ſhall be heard : that Miniſter ſhall be told of the beggarly ſtate of the wretched in a tone as intelligible as that he practiſed before he was Miniſter, and before he was Member for Cambridge, when he harangued at the Revolution Society for parliamentary reforms, which now, alas, are diſcuſſed by him no more !

A man in office and out of office is like a player in comedy and tragedy. In office he aſſumes a cheerful countenance, characteriſes pleaſant comedy, promiſes, flatters, and careſſes his ſuitors—out of office, he rants, threatens, and talks of vice and corruption, the ax; the block, and the Tower. Reformation will never come from a Miniſter—come when it will, it will be from the people.

I hope there is not one who thinks becauſe money is plenty—the funds are high and the lottery wheel goes round—that the poor are the better for it, or their vices abated. If additional wealth operated in any manner upon the vicious, it would be by increaſing their enormities— Gold reforms not the corrupted heart.

The labourer who has conſumed his ſtrength by active toil, and can no longer earn his bread, will not be benefited by the increaſed wealth of another—if he can compound with the iron heart

of

of an overfeer, and preferve his cot and his blanket whilft he receives his pittance from the parifh, the fummit of his expectation is perfect.

The pauper that is paffed from London to Cornwall or Northumberland, may finifh his journey of life upon the road, without the fhelter of any thing better than a barn—Will he be benefited by the riches that he fees in his journey, by the difplay of fmooth lawns, grand manfions, and profperous towns?

Will Mr. Wilberforce fay that thefe confiderations do not fpeak home to the human heart more than the condition of negroes?—If not, I will prefent him with a catalogue of human diftrefs pofitively exifting in this land of freedom, and I will invite him to compare the ftate of thoufands in this country with that of the negroes in the Weft-Indies.

What is a *foldier* but a flave? Does any one pretend to fay that his ftate of flavery is not neceffary? that in the chain of fociety he does not form a link? But yet he is a flave, becaufe he is bound to certain duties, and cannot with any change of mind extricate himfelf from bondage. As long as he is content and does his duty, he feels not the galling of the yoke; but as foon as he is rebellious, he is whipped, placed upon fpikes, chained, imprifoned, and fometimes fhot. Perhaps he was enlifted under the influence of intoxication—perhaps under that of defperation—

perhaps

perhaps he is ordered abroad, away from his
wife and family---will the four-pence a day ferve
him if he ftay at home, or provide for his wife
and children in his abfence? And if under this
pretence he afks for his freedom, is it granted?

If it be faid that the *foldier's* punifhment is
not more fevere than that of the *negroe*, I do
contradict it: the foldier often lingers under repeated flagellations; and an inftance has lately
occurred of one who put an end to his mifery by
fuicide who was to have undergone this correction the third time.

Will any man fay that the Weft-India planter
is not as much interefted in humanity for his
flave as the commander of a regiment for his?
Let Mr. Wilberforce, by anfwering the queftion,
fill up the blank.

Commerce and an infular fituation invite failors. They go their voyages with the fongs by
heart that chaunt the joys at their return. At
Deal, or fometimes before they defcry the white
cliffs that proclaim the land of promifed hope,
they are tied and bound and configned to the
difcipline of a man of war. It is vain that we
are told they are *better off*; no one can believe it;
it cannot be fo, or they would go without compulfion; and it is that very compulfion which is
another word for flavery: flaves they are as long
as the war lafts, or their ftrength holds out.
Greenwich Hofpital receives not a thoufandth
part

part of them. The endearments of life, which
are love and affection, by that time are all become extinct: but this, in a land of freedom,
forms a *neceſſary* link in the chain of ſociety.

I ſay nothing of *kidnapping to the Eaſt-Indies—
I have been only told that ſuch a thing is.* But the
flocks of mutilated beggars in ſailor's habits that
haunt the ſtreets and public roads, prove what
the humanity of government is towards them
when their ſervices are paſt. Ay, ſays Mr. Wilberforce, the laws protect the Engliſhman againſt
the kidnapper; ſo ſay I; but he who was kidnapped muſt firſt be reſtored: the laws alſo in
the Weſt-Indies protect the negroes.

The buſineſs of an Adminiſtration ſeems to be
nothing more than to lay on taxes and extract
them from the people. If protection be aſked,
if poverty appeal, the tax-gatherer becomes the
judge: the poor inhabitant who is not provided
to pay his tax upon the third call, is threatened
with a ſummary proceſs; and the money which
he ſcrapes together perhaps to his laſt ſhilling,
is a part of that ſurplus which is made up for the
jubilee day of finance. But this is alſo a *neceſſary*
link in the chain of ſociety. All cannot climb
to the ſummit of the hill of fortune; ſome tire in
the aſcent, ſome dare not the attempt, ſome fall
down in the purſuit, and are trampled to death.

The great burthen of taxes, and the wide diftinction betwixt the rich and the poor, oblige
the

the latter to be flavifh to the former. There are many objects in inclement feafons without an hovel and with fcarcely any covering, that tempt humanity in the road from *York* to London— Thefe might be feen and their miferies might be told from their own mouths, if Mr. Wilberforce beftowed the fame portion of humanity towards them that he has to the tales of a difcarded over-feer from the Weft-Indies.

Will Mr. Wilberforce, and thofe who join iffue with him in the caufe of the abolition of the Slave-Trade, confent to examine as many witneffes who are competent to inform a Committee of the vices and the miferies of the loweft clafs of people at home—print the Reports—and make the compa-rifon fairly with thofe of the flaves in the Weft-Indies—not only as to pofitive conditions of diftrefs, but alfo to numbers—not only fuch con-ditions as are *neceffary* for making the public wheel go round—but fuch as are the refult of wanton inattention, cruelty, and inhumanity? Will *they* enquire into the number of dram-fhops, and afcertain the clafs of people who frequent them? will they do the fame with the publick-houfes? will they fearch out the haunts of thieves that are not taken? will they afcertain the caufe and the haunts of beggars? will they enquire into the caufe of increafe of the parochial taxes, and revife the poor laws? will they obtain reports from the manufacturing towns of the

prefent

prefent ftate of the weavers, and from *Cornwall*
and *Durham* of that of the miners and colliers ?
will they examine into the cafes of prifoners
confined for debt, and diftinguifh guilt from
misfortune ? will they relieve the miferable ftate
of thoufands that *cannot dig, but are aſhamed to
beg?* will they fully convince the world that
fome do not fink from pofitive want—that fome
do not die of the fmall pox who might have been
preferved ? will they examine into the caufe of
the prefent rage for new prifons, and will they
prove to us that thefe new walls are unneceffary ?
will they ftop the hands of the mafon, turn the
forged irons into ploughfhares, and pay off a
part of the national debt by favings in the ex-
pences of *Botany Bay?*

When thefe reforms are proved to be neceffary, and when they are carried into effect, the
eye of humanity may penetrate and difcover de-
fects in remoter regions, and pour forth the heal-
ing balm of comfort to relieve them. The rifing
fun, which we all adore becaufe of its univerfal
benignity—*firft* gladdens the hills neareft to the
horizon—it is *afterwards* that its rays are extended to remoter parts. We may defcend to
the rank of the wretched in *England*, but cannot
to that in *Africa.*

In the comparative operations upon the human
mind, tragedies which reprefent domeftic diftrefs
engage the attention more than thofe of the fates

of tyrants or deftruction of empires—fcenes are more moving, as reprefenting to the auditor what he would himfelf feel, if he were to do or to fuffer what is there feigned to be fuffered or to be done.   The reflexion which ftrikes home to the heart is that they are conditions to which *ourfelves* may be expofed—we lament the poffibility as a mother weeps over the babe when fhe remem- bers that death may take it from her.

On Comparative Slavery.

HAVING fomewhat enlarged my fentiments upon humanity, and expanded the purpofes of it that it may be feen more clearly and diftinguifhed more readily from that which is refembling to humanity—but is only the counterfeit; I fhall proceed upon the fame fyftem in imparting my fentiments upon Comparative Slavery.

There are many more pofitive conditions of *flavery* than that of one man being the property of another, and being fubject to his will and dominion : and if fuch pofitive conditions be *neceffary* in every affociation of men, both under a civilifed government as ftates but little removed from that of nature—if various ranks and orders of men be *neceffary*, that the political wheel may go round, that the purpofes of focial life be more completely fulfilled—if it be pofitively according with the natural order of things—why then there cannot be a doubt remaining but that, *the only duty is to make all occupations and all conditions of men as comfortable as the nature of their ftations will admit.*

This pofition ought either to be received as a general maxim, or not at all—either as an incumbent duty which the dependant in every ftate may claim at the hands of their fuperiors, or not

at

at all. For if it be not a right, but only an optional caprice, the impreffion of it would be fo
light that the tint could not be traced, and it
would be better for the dependant clafs to be left
to ftruggle againft their own fufferings than to
depend upon any fuch precarious bounty; and
in the language of the Poet at once to be told—

> Why let the ftrucken deer go weep
> The hart ungalled play—
> For fome muft watch, whilft fome muft fleep :—
> So runs the world away!

The pofitive wants of life in fome climates are
very few indeed; and when thefe are gratified
with the mind at eafe, it is very immaterial towards human happinefs into whofe hands the
furplus may fall.

Whether a negro *flave* or a Ruffian *flave*—
a Pruffian foldier or an Anfpacher—an Englifh
foldier or a failor—a peafant or a collier—provided their pofitive wants be fupplied and they
chearfully purfue their occupations, it would be
vain in reformation to grant them more.

For if men thus conditioned could not look
up with chearful faces to the ftations of their
fuperiors, and if it were not certain that true
happinefs was not confined to redundant wealth
and power, the proportion of human wretchednefs would be greatly extended indeed;—it
would be a difeafe of the mind which no reform

7   could

could cure, becaufe all cannot poffefs wealth and dominion : and where we now find willing obedience, we fhould then fee nothing but envy, rancour, and revenge.

If he be only happy who is moft free, the peafant in England is the happieft. But why then does he become a foldier and a *flave ?*—becaufe he valued not that freedom, and was not content. Why, when he is a foldier, does he wifh to become a peafant—to have reftored to him again his former condition and his furrendered privilege ?—Not at the time perhaps that he was enlifted—not as long as the paffion for the parade, the drum and the fife, charms him—but when he fickens at thefe—it is *then,* and *not till then,* that he finds himfelf a pofitive *flave.*

A peafant has the lighteft burthen of cares, and ftands firm upon that level in life which will not admit of fudden and violent fhocks from fortune.

If the peafant becomes miferable—if he at any time of life approaches to that ftate which is as bad as pofitive *flavery*—there cannot be any difficulty in affigning the caufe for it, becaufe all the poffible ones are but few. Either his fcene of content was difturbed by war or immorality when in the prime of his life, or his daily hard toil is ever hardly rewarded.

If

If he marry, (and moſt of the peaſants do), he finds that his wages will not ſupport himſelf and his increaſing family. It is then that he feels himſelf a *ſlave* in another ſenſe—a *ſlave* in a comparative degree worſe than a negro poſ-ſeſſed of the ſame will, the ſame induſtry, and the ſame number of children.

The peaſant muſt divide and ſubdivide his ſhilling. His very farthings will admit of frac-tions. His cot is rented—his firing muſt be purchaſed—his ſickneſs muſt be ſupported at his own expence—his cloathing for himſelf and fa-mily muſt be bought by himſelf. But if he cannot by œconomy procure theſe poſitive ne-ceſſaries, he perhaps then will apply to his pariſh. The new coat that he purchaſed for the wedding day, will be the laſt that he can ever buy ! Juſt as much will be apportioned out to him from his pariſh as will keep his body and ſoul together.—If he cannot do the work of an able labourer, his pay is diminiſhed, and the pariſh conſiders that in their bounty.

It is neceſſary, for the ſake of my compariſon, to take notice—that the peaſant is alſo amenable to the criminal laws of his country—that if he ſteals a turnip*, gets a baſtard, breaks down a fence,

* I myſelf ſaw a man who received the contents of a gun charged with ſmall ſhot in his breaſt. The affair happened at twelve o'clock at noon : the man died the ſame night, and there

fence, poaches a hare, or commits any other fe-
lonious act or fraud—there are ftocks, whips, and
heavy fetters, *in England for him*, as there are *in
the Weft Indies for the negro.*

He that vifits the villages in England, and
contemplates the condition of the peafantry in
general, if he take Goldfmith's Deferted Village
in his hand, he will be enabled to afcertain whether poetry be all a fiction, and for once he will
be fo unfortunate as to vouch that in this inftance it is faithfully realifed.

I have paffed three years of my life in the
Weft-Indies, and practifed phyfick there during
that time. I had the care of two thoufand negroes annually. Before I proceed to fpeak of
the condition of negroes, as I found it, I will
obtrude upon my reader one obfervation,
which is, that ever fince my return from the
Weft-Indies, and before the fubject of *flavery*
had been agitated, I have been ever heard to
fay—that fo widely different were the conditions
of a good field negro and a good peafant, that
if it were my lot to be reduced to the choice of
being the one or the other, I fhould without
hefitation prefer the ftate of the negro to that of
the peafant.

I have

---

there was an end of the matter. It was done by a watchman
in a turnip field near London, and the man who was fhot was
drawing a few. He was brought to the Middlefex Hofpital
in the year 1765.

I have ftated the general condition of the peafant, and now I will ftate the general condition
of the negro.   If I fwerve from the truth, I do
not look for my punifhment from men.

A good field negro has his hut and his planting ground—his hogs and his poultry—which
he may either eat or fell.   Thefe are on the
fame eftate where his labour is employed.   For
the hut and the ground he pays no rent—he has
the neceffary cloathing found him.   But he is
not content with that—he is able to purchafe
good linen for fhirts and trowfers and jackets—
He lives in a climate where, in the language of
a poet, *the fun always fhines*—that climate is
perfectly congenial to his nature.   His wife or
his children do not draw from him their necef-
faries of life—neither food or raiment—When
any of them are fick, they are carefully attended
without any expence, and they are provided
with every comfort which their condition re-
quires.   His toil is fo light that he feels it not—
his freedom is fo indifferent to him that he will
not buy it—but it is in the power of every good
negro to be rich enough for procuring it, if he
chofe to exchange his condition.   He has no
other concern upon his mind but that of pre-
ferving the good-will of his mafter.   In de-
fcending into the vale of life, no reflections of
poverty ftrike home to his heart; and when his
days of labour are counted, he ftill receives his
                                        allow-

allowance, cultivates his planting ground, raifes his tobacco, and enjoys the reft of his days un-der the fhade of his own *Banana* tree. If his mafter's fortune fhould turn out adverfe, and his eftate be fold, the property of the negroe, both in money and ftock, remains untouched by the mafter's creditors.

It is impoffible for a good peafant to have the pofitive comforts of a good field negroe : the fevereft labour that he undergoes, and which is only for a few months in the year, is that of digging cane holes—the labour of a gardener is to the full as exceffive.

The reft of his labour is a mere play game.

He is not expofed to be dragged away by a prefs gang, nor inveigled by a recruiting fer-jeant : it is a million to one but he falls, like a tree, on the fame fpot where he firft grew into life, and that he dies in that hut which he him-felf erected.

But what if he be turned over to another maf-ter---what if he be removed from one eftate to another?---Is there any thing fo formidable in that ?--.If there be, how is it that peafants in England change their mafters every *quartêr* of a year ?

The good field negroe carries with him his own character : every body will know him wherever he goes or whomfoever he ferves un-der. Strokes of the cart whip raife the

F fkin—

skin—fetters gall it : if he has neither whelks
or galls—and none he will have, becaufe he has
not deferved them····he is known every where to
be a good negroe.

I fmile at the nonfenfe of thofe who can imagine that the Weft-Indian would treat his negroe
with inhumanity, that he would be fo loft to
that intereft which the reft of fociety fteadily
adheres to. The *cart whip*, the *chains*, and the
ftocks, are to a good negroe what engines of
punifhment are to a good man in every fociety—
for his protection.

The queftion, I truft, will no longer be, whether
the negroe be the only *flave*, but whether his
ftate of *flavery* be the beft or the worft of all
thofe whom fortune has placed and whom *neceffity* continues in a ftate of dependance. The
queftion, I truft alfo, will no longer be, whether
thefe fubordinate conditions be pofitively neceffary in all ftates or not, for *they moft affuredly
are*, and are proved to be fo, fince they are
found in every ftate, and no one could go on
without them ; the principal link in the chain of
fociety would be otherwife broken.

As no ftate can difpenfe with the foldier, the
vaffal, the peafant, or the *flave*, which are all
fynonymous, which are only fo many words ex-
preffing the fame meaning, fo every ftate is
bound to protect them, to treat them with the
kindeft humanity, and in return for their labour

to fupply their wants *from the moment they draw their firſt breath to their final expiration.*

In northern climates the pofitive wants are greater than in fouthern. In that fituation where nature has diftributed moſt laviſhly her bounties, leſs is left to be fupplied by the hands of power. The negroe, in this view of the queftion, enjoys many preferable advantages.

If I make an enlarged furvey of Europe, all of which might be confidered to be in a ftate of civilifation, I ſhall find that, befides peafants, vaffals, and failors on board men of war, Europe contains more than two million of foldiers. The whole of the lower claſs of people in Ruffia are in a ftate of vaffalage. Fanaticks who rave for the freedom of a negroe, poffibly do not know this, for fanaticifm and ignorance generally go together : but if they ſhould not have known it *biſtorically*, they might perhaps have read in an Englifh *newſpaper* that the Emprefs of Ruffia now and then beftows a large tract of land *with a competent number of vaſſals* in rewarding the meritorious deeds of her ftatefmen and officers*.

Are thefe conditions, in fuch a climate as from the fouthern continent of Germany to the

* When I was in Ruffia I faw forty criminals chained together, and thus crawling through the ſtreets of St. Peterſburgh. But if any one doubts of the cruelties exiſting in Europe, I refer him to Mr. Howard's ftate of their prifons.

frozen

frozen regions of Kampſkatka, preferable to
that of negroes in the Weſt-Indies protected by
maſters verſed in the practice of *humanity?* The
Prince of Heſſe and Margrave of Anſpach hired
out their ſoldiers to Britain during its war with
America: they were ſent acroſs the Atlantick
to fight thoſe battles in which their provocations
had no concern—they there added to, and mixed
in that deluge of carnage, without an atom of
the impulſe of nature and freedom—they were
bound to fight there for Britain, as they would
have been, if their rulers commanded it, any
where elſe againſt her—If their rulers were
paid, it is immaterial as to any other *cauſe—*
they would make for *that* an alliance with the
Ruſſian—with the Turk—or with the *Devil* himſelf, if his dominion were upon earth.

I am perfectly convinced, and therefore do
not heſitate to declare the fact, that the peaſantry
of this country were *throughout* their lives a happier claſs of men—that they began and ended
their days with leſs poſitive diſtreſs—and that
they experienced fewer wants—when they were
under the protection of the *Barons* than ſince
that protection has been withdrawn—that their
toil was not ſo great, and their comforts greater,
They have now no other relation in ſociety but
only as long as they are able to work; when that
power is conſumed, *all is now over with them.*

In

In the days of the *Barons* they paid nothing for their cots nor for their fuel. A common was allotted to every village; they reared their own flock; and with thefe fupports *old age*, grown too feeble for labour, could advance without the companion of *defpair* or *the dread of an overfeer.*

I know the hiftory of my country too well to be told that the peafantry, of their own accord, fhook off their ftate of vaffalage to the *Barons.* They did not—it was by feduction that they were brought to it—it was in the ftruggle betwixt the *King* and the *Barons* that they exchanged their conditions, and God forbid that I fhould fay they were now mended.

If the vaffal went to the war, it was that fort of warfare which can only be juftified : he fought in his own caufe, as well as that of his mafter : he fought *pro aris et focis*, and equally partook of the infult and revenge. Some *foul feducer* then ftirred up difcontent among them, as ano-ther would now among the negroes, with this wide difference, that in the laft inftance there is neither political caufe or natural connection to juftify the feduction.

If I were to extend my enquiry throughout the known habitable globe, my argument on the predominant comparative mifery of others with that of the negroes in the Weft-Indies would be yet more ftrongly enforced; but as I might be told that the *mines of Peru* belong not to us,

and

and therefore thofe who dig in them come not
within our pale of humanity, I fhall leave their
conditions to be difcovered through the fame
telefcope and by the fame philofophers who
have explored the coafts of Africa, traverfed the
middle paffage, and realifed vifionary monfters
for cruelty in the Weft-India iflands.

But I recommend them to turn their attention,
by way of relief, to the miners in *Cornwall* and
colliers in *Durham.* On the day of their report,
I hope to hear from them that the accommodations of thofe *neceffary* members in fociety are
comfortably fitting for all feafons of the year—
that becaufe they are working on Englifh
ground, and partaking of Englifh freedom, they
enjoy good Englifh food—and that when they
are paft their labour they find a moft hofpitable
retreat—that thefe damps from the caves of the
earth which have *blafted hundreds at once,* blaft
now no more—and that the conditions of thofe
need no commiferation who never revifit the
glimpfes of the fun or moon.

At any rate I do not fuppofe that the miners
in *England* are worfe off-than the miners in
Sweden or thofe in *Ruffia,* and that is fome
confolation to your modern philanthropift.

Now that I have given a fketch of the comparative ftate of thofe in active induftry in Europe, and who in their relation to fociety form
the fame link or ftand on the fame level with the
negroe of the Weft-Indies, I fhall not beg leave,
but

but will take the liberty of calling the attention of my reader to another clafs of *flavery* which is below all comparifon, and which is more poignantly felt becaufe the objects have fallen from a greater height and experienced the feverer fhock from their great reverfe of fortune.

This enquiry can be more ftrictly purfued in England, by pointing out the conditions of thoufands *there imprifoned*, than by extending that enquiry beyond thofe white cliffs which bound *the ifland of liberty.*

Why at this moment of time thefe thoufands are thus immured within the confines of a prifon for *debts* is not difficult to be accounted for, but it is difficult to affign a juft reafon why they ought.

The phyfical caufe of their getting there is certainly owing to the commercial enterprife of the people—not to their *liberality* in giving credit, but to their *avarice* after profit.

There never was a country known in hiftory where the fortune of man—where his *ups* and his *downs*, ran round upon the wheel in more rapid revolutions—Then why fhould a fingle Englifhman be fhut out of his chance in this privileged lottery in life, and why fhould he that is *down*, be prevented from *rifing again?* What mental improvement, what corporeal ftrength, what active induftry, does he acquire who is fhut up within the walls of a prifon? What intellectual fatisfaction or virtuous reform

6

can be derived from incarcerating the body, and
making it a dead weight upon a ftate ? It is
more liking to *a viper biting the file* than to any
thing like reafon. It is very rare indeed that
another fuch as *Sir Walter Raleigh* mingles in
that fcene, and who *in his prifon hours like him
can enrich the world.*

When Mr. Wilberforce again revives the fubject of *flavery*, I will endeavour to prevail upon
fome friends in the Houfe of Commons to afk
him if this be not *flavery* with a vengeance—
flavery in the very practice. I think it was Lord
Rawdon who faid within this week in the Houfe
of Lords, that a woman had been confined for
twenty-five years for a debt of twenty pounds.

> —— Turn thy complexion there——
> Patience, thou young and rofe-lipp'd cherubin !

There is a wide diftinction betwixt *flavery* put
into practice and the power of doing it—betwixt the condition which exacts *active obedience* and that which is configned to *paffive fuf-
fering.*

He who is fubjected to the will of a mafter
might pafs the whole of his life without feeling
the leaft of that power ; and if he abide within
the pale of duty might not fmart from the tugs
of authority ; the cord about his neck might
hang loofely and the habit of wearing it become
                                    familiar,

familiar, but the poor wretch immured in a prifon is in a ftate of *pofitive flavery*; and whether he be young or old, active or lazy, he is yet in a ftate of *paffive exiftence.*

The penal laws of this country are too fhocking to be read. Every multiplication of them is an additional circle more contracted than a former trefpaffing upon the rights of man in civil fociety.

The Roman Catholicks are reftricted in fo many ways, that they can only be defined to be *flaves* permitted to walk at large—they can neither purchafe land, carry a gun, act as jurymen, vote at an election, ferve in parliament, or prefide in any office—the law hangs over them, like a fufpended fword by a thread:—but under all thefe reftraints as long as they keep within that pale which the law has marked out for them, they pafs through life without a fenfe of pain.

That muft be faid to be a reform in religion which conveys *no traits* of *him* who founded it: it was not prefcribed by him that the various fects of chriftianity fhould be fubject to the tyranny of an eftablifhed one—that becaufe one fect cannot in confcience fit down in the pew of another, but is willing to be free in fitting in a pew of its own—it is to be marked, perfecuted, and become the victim of tumult.

G   The

The laft pamphlet on *negroe flavery* was written by a divine* of the Church of England, by
one who has feen lately in filence, *Englifhmen
galley flaves at Morocco*, where he dwelt for
fome time and witneffed the miferies inflicted.
This pamphlet was written in confequence of the
tumults at *St. Domingo*, the news of which
reached *England* at the immediate time of the
riots at *Birmingham*; but the fufferers here have
found no fuch pen in the hands of a clergyman
to commifferate their ruin—no tongue to plead
it where protection is a duty. *Dr. Prieftley*,
ever active, both fuffers and acts; he is the com-
mentator of his own and the misfortunes of his
fellow fufferers—like another *Zenophon*, by re-
cording his loffes and his fuccefsful retreat from
the hands of his favage fpoilers, he has approved
his philofophy and elevation of mind.

As a fellow citzen I am more anxious to
know what paffed at *Birmingham* than I can be
fuppofed to be at *St. Domingo*. But Mr. Wilberforce has not as yet fharpened his humanity
for our *civil* broils: upon that point he is as
cold as a Stoick.

I have not forgotten the following anec-
dote of him: during the long conteft in the
Weftminfter election—when Sir Cecil Wray oppofed Mr. Fox—every day produced riots—

many

* Percival Stockdale.

many were wounded—but one was *murdered*. In confequence of this Mr. Fox, on the firſt day of the meeting of the new parliament, com-plained to the Houſe of the foulneſs of that oppoſition which was made againſt him and gave a detail of the tranſactions that had paſſed. Mr. Wilberforce replied to him; and ended his ſpeech with the following piece of ſtoiciſm— " That he (Mr. Fox) had better prove to the Houſe that he had a fair majority of votes, and produce ſome ſubſtantial arguments why the ſcrutiny ſhould not be continued, inſtead of en-tertaining the Houſe with *horrid tales of blood and maſſacre.*"

This was Mr. Wilberforce in the year 1784!

What is become of Mr. Gilbert's bill for a Reform in the *poor laws of England?* Does it lie upon the ſame table with the papers on the *African Slave Trade*—or is it thrown aſide to give room for the latter?—or are they both to be bound up in one volume, and preſerved in order to point out the contraſt?

What is to be the fate of Sir William Dol-ben's Motion in favour of the *proſtitutes* who apply in the ſtreets from Whitechapel to Hyde Park Corner? Could there not be found a ſuf-ficient number in the Houſe to ſtand up in ſup-port of thoſe miſerable outcaſts? Did ſuch a theme excite neither curioſity or humanity? Was it not ſomething to have known how ſuch

as are young in the practice of luſt were conducted to theſe haunts, and how the ſupply of
youth, beauty, and decoration was furniſhed
in ſuch ſucceſſions? how they were ſeduced—
how they were lodged—and what became of
them when they were diſeaſed? If theſe girls
were examined and the bawds detected, there
would be proved a traffick *worthy* the inveſti-
gation of *humanity.*

It is incumbent upon the Houſe of Commons
to take up this cauſe, ſeeing that the *Police* of
Weſtminiſter is ſo looſe and ſo proſtituted. It
is the higheſt inſult upon common ſenſe to be
,told that *Government* cares for the morals of
the people or for the promotion of their induſtry—It is in the abuſe of either that all their pre-
ſent *freedom* conſiſts, and it is *Government* who
ſupplies their very temptations.

There can be but one reaſon aſſigned why
an inquiry into the miſeries and vices of the low-
eſt claſs of people in *England* is thus neglected,
and why in the *Weſt-Indies* it is ſo induſtriouſly
purſued—and this is the Reaſon—

The atrocious facts in the very Boſom of this
country are *not ſeen* becauſe they are the moſt
obvious, and are not inveſtigated becauſe the
government is *directly* reſponſible for them—
whereas the grievances ſuppoſed to be exiſting
in the *Weſt-Indies,* either on the part of the
maſter or the *ſlave,* are remote from ſight, and for
the

the redrefs of which the Government of this country is not *directly* refponfible.

England poffeffes the *Weft-Indies* as a fovereignty, and might have an ultimate power there : But be it remembered that there is a code of laws and a legiflative power on every ifland in the *Weft-Indies.* For whatever abufes that have paffed uncorrected the *legiflature there* are *directly* refponfible. Let this country proceed therefore in its *plan of confiftency*; and fince it appears more rational in *Government* to follow up the inquiry in the *Weft-Indies* and neglect it *at home,*—let it perfift as it has began, in paffing the cenfure *before* it has attached the criminality, and in *keeping the beam* in its own eye the *better to difcern a mote* in another's.

On *the African Slave Trade.*

IT is neceffary to remark that the *Slave Trade*
firft was began and has been ever fince continued by the fubjects of this country—that it
never was, from its firft commencement, either
a fmuggling or a kidnapping trade—but that it
always has been a trade pofitively under the
fanction of the *laws of this country*, and in
which the *Weft-India planters* never had any
other concern than that of purchafing thofe
negroes which the Englifh acts of parliament
fent to their iflands.

It is neceffary alfo to remark, that the Weft-
India iflands were taken by Englifh fleets and
that the adventurers on Weft-India property on
thofe iflands were chiefly *ab origines* of England.

It would be idle to fay that thefe adventurers
would have renounced their native homes without a profpect of enlarging their property by
induftry, and it would be as idle to fay that
they ever could have obtained that end without
their having been, *at leaft till now*, encouraged
in the means.

Inftead of the *Weft-India planters* having
fuggefted the mode of traffick after they firft
fettled in the iflands, it was the traffick that
fuggefted their fettlement there. From h e

reign

reign of *Elizabeth* to that of *George the Third*, the laws of *African Traffick* have been in force. Ships have embarked from England to the coasts of Africa and exchanged English produce for what was offered by the Africans. Besides gold dust, ivory, &c. there were offered *prisoners taken in war—criminals*—such negroes as the mode of African government had judged *to be sacrificed to their laws.*

Whether their laws were human or inhuman I will not now take upon me to say. If they were inhuman and such as we in a more civilised state ought to have been shocked at—or ought to have renounced—we then have taken a very long space of time for ripening our humanity. Our humanity was either long in planting or long in growing.—From the reign of Elizabeth to that of George the Third there has been one continued blight on its blossoms—some noxious pestilence has all along destroyed the delicious fruit—the tree has never yet borne that which was meet to be poured into the bitter cup of the African as a balm to his adversity and a sweet remembrancer to his future hope of happier days!

If during a space of 150 years our ancestors had recoiled at the *traffick of human flesh,* (be the motive founded in humanity or not)—how happened it that in the various wars in which this country has been since engaged, the policy

of

of it has been to extend our poffeffions in the
Weft-Indies, knowing as it always did—that
the more thefe poffeffions were extended, the
greater would be the demand for thofe who
can alone cultivate them.

During the *arbitrary reigns* of the *Stuarts*,
fhoals of emigrants left this land of difcontent;
and if *European labourers* had chofen to cultivate in the fugar iflands—to take the hoe out
of the hands of the negroes—they would fome
of them have fettled *on them* when the whole
went for *America.*

Or if the idea had been practicable and
choice for preferable labour had been out of
the queftion, *Government* might have configned thofe tranfports to the *Weft-Indies* it
fent to *America:*—thofe tranfports which have
added to the population of a country—which
have fince fuccefsfully rebelled and trium-
phantly fhook off fubjection to the pofterity of
their *judges* who fent them into exile.

In our wars that proclaimed our conquefts—
and not fuch as our laft—in the war that was
concluded juft after the acceffion of *George the
Third*—when we poffeffed the vaft continent
of *America*—when we were nearly one hundred
millions lefs in debt—when *neceffity* was not
choice and the world was all before us where to
chufe—how happened it that even then no
fuggeftion of the *Slave Trade* being founded
                                              in

in inhumanity occupied a corner in the hearts of *Englishmen?*

Goree and *Senegal* became ours in that war. Proofs could have then found their way to the Commons of England without an appeal to a *Liverpool Captain,* a *Swedish Botanist,* or an *African Governor.* The whole of a Britifh fleet with a *Keppel* their commander, rode *there* triumphant. For fo valuable a conqueft, the ftreamers were fpread to the winds—and the voice of mifery—the cries of murder—or the tale of kidnapping, would never have affailed his *ears* without a ready reparation from his *heart.*

Was there any word like inhumanity to be read in that *Gazette* which announced the glory of taking *Goree?* If there were, the operation of it upon the minds of Englifhmen *then* was moft ftrangely reverfe to what it would be *now*—For the *canons* from the *Tower—bonfires* and *illuminations* proved it to be a conqueft of great importance—glorious as a victory—advantageous as a fettlement—and reflecting additional wealth to *Great Britain* by extending the cultivation of fugar in the *Weft-Indies.*

Liverpool nor *Briftol* has any thing to anfwer for by having carried on an *African* commerce. The fituation of both was the moft favourable for the commerce. The merchants there find their juftification in having obeyed acts of par-

H   liament.

liament. If the *African Slave Trade* be criminal, it is notwithſtanding an *act* of *Government*—and *Government* is now *judge, criminal,* and *accuſer.* The crimes, if any have been perpetrated in procuring *ſlaves* from the coaſt of *Africa,* are all the reſult of acts of parliament.

There was a time when a reformation, for the ſake of *humanity,* would have come before the publick with a better grace—when that which cannot be now an act of neceſſity, was once an act of choice—when England was leſs taxed and the national debt not ſwollen to ſuch an enormity—when the conſequences of the abolition would not have excited another concern left for the decreaſe of two million of annual revenue ariſing from the *Weſt-Indies,* an increaſe could not be deviſed by any means upon the property of *this country* to ſupply the deficiency.

Burthened as this country now is—hemmed in by taxes on every way we turn—reminded in every intercourſe of the national load by impoſts of every ſort—incapable of reading, looking, taſting, riding, paying, or receiving, without taxation—is this a time for liſtening to the conditions of *others,* or even to be harraſſed afreſh with reflexions on our *own ?*

Are individuals the richer becauſe enough can be barely extracted from them for keeping a clear annual ſcore with the national debt ?

Are

Are they in a temper for having their paffions difturbed from a peaceful attention towards induftry by twopenny pamphlets circulated from houfe to houfe—dreffed up with a partial intention of ftirring up the feelings by paffages felected for the purpofe ?

If the traffick be inhuman and if the publick at large are to be appealed to—let the whole of the truth be feen by them and let them not *be tricked out of their humanity by inflammatory extracts.*

Let the four numbers which are entitled
" *Abridgements on the Minutes of the Evidence*
" taken before a Committee of the whole
" Houfe of Commons, to whom it was referred
" to confider of the *Slave Trade* in the years
" 1789, 1790, and 1791," be circulated with that *fame* induftry that the moft inflammable paffages felected out of them have been—let the appeal be made to the *reafon* of Englilhmen and not to the *paffion.*

And let them then, in addition to what they will find in the *Abridgements* of *Evidence,* be told of the caufe which *firft* eftablilhed the *trade in Africa*—that fuch negroes which were received on board Englilh veffels would have been *facrificed* to the laws of their country if not thus redeemed and refcued by commerce— and let them be told that it was that confide-

H 2 ration

ration which firſt infpired that principle of commerce there.

If from the beginning abufes have crept in—
if the firſt principle be fomewhat changed—if
the *African chiefs* do *now* contrive means for
increaſing the *African captives,* through the
temptation of barter—if that which was the
effect of humanity be now the caufe in fome
meafure of *ſlavery*—if the baneful influence of
intoxicating ſpirits has perverted the natural
courfe of *African juſtice,* by which more negroes are driven into captivity than have forfeited otherwife their freedom and their lives—
If this be the cafe, does it follow from hence
that there are no other negroes put on board
than what are procured by the *criminality* of
their chiefs—that the original caufe has totally
ceafed—and that if the influence of *intoxication*
were withdrawn, there would now be found *no*
negroes who had forfeited their lives to the
juſtice of their country and who would be put
to death if not *refcued* and *preferved* by European commerce ?

I could be brought to believe that the cafe
may be fo in an *Arcadian paradiſe,* if that was
realifed which fancy has only fuggefted, but I
know not that country in the four quarters of
the globe which does not punifh criminals
without affigning the caufe to the *intoxication* of
judges.

If

If the truth of the cafe could poffibly be, that the temptation of *fpirituous liquors* fupported folely the *African Slave Trade*—if this were pofitively the fact, and the whole of the African queftion turns upon it—if negroes cannot be received on board Britifh fhips without inhuman temptation on the part of *Britons,* and if that were the fole caufe of their being *driven* into captivity and *fold* into bondage—*then ought fuch a traffick no longer to exift.* If this were pofitively the cafe, any future eftablifhment of a fubfequent fact—that the negroes on their arrival in the *Weft-Indies* are much better provided with every means of human happinefs, than they could have found in their *native* foil, in my opinion would be unworthily contended for; their being *kidnapped* away and *robbed* of their freedom—as the *Englifh foldiers* are alfo faid to be to the *Eaft-Indies*—and not having *forfeited* their freedom, will admit of no palliation—not even that of ftate *neceffity.*

But this has not been proved to be the principal caufe of the African flavery—*Witchcraft, Gaming, Thieving, Adultery,* and *War,* were the original caufes, and by the uniform evidence of Englifh witneffes who beft underftand the laws and cuftoms of *Africans,* proofs are brought home to our conviction that thefe fame caufes do exift at the *prefent* time. This fact the following extracts will confirm beyond a doubt.

" If

" *If prifoners cannot ranfom themfelves—
" muft be fold—they have a power over pri-
" foners of war in the act of capture—that but
" for flavery the laws would be more fan-
" guinary—that during war flaves were cheapeft.

" Trials for witchcraft generally in the night:
" but from generally feeing all fatisfied, except
" the culprits, concludes the trials fair—Princi-
" pals in witchcraft are facrificed—the reft fold
" to flavery. Commonly the whole family
" fuffer flavery, but with fome exceptions."

" † Convicts are generally confined till fold.
" He who receives a flave, in exchange for a
" convict, may ufe him as he pleafes : he may
" fell him to the Europeans. Convicts for
" witchcraft are generally put to death as vic-
" tims, immediately after the fentence. Trials
" for witchcraft being fecret in the night, their
" fituation can be known only from the fellers
" or the convicts, who not confidering it dif-
" graceful, make no fecret of what they were
" fold for.

" There was a ferious war between the *Fan-
" tees* and *Afhantees*, the two moft powerful
" nations we know of, fhortly after his arrival,
" for a year or more. It was an inland war,
" caufed by the *Afhantees* wifhing for part of
" the coaft—thinks he can confidently fay it
" was

* Barnes, N? I. Abridgment of Evidence, &c. from page 1
to page 9.
† Miles, N? I. from page 9 to page 18.

" was not caufed or prolonged for making
" flaves—conceives that many were fold for
" theft—fewer for adultery—and the feweft for
" debt.

" *Slavery is univerfal, the flaves very nume-
" rous fometimes. Bought by Europeans from
" the native keepers between thofe who bring
" them from inland and the fhips—he appre-
" hends nine tenths of the flaves come from
" inland, the other one tenth from the fmall
" diftrict on the beach—that they were made
" flaves for adultery, witchcraft, theft, and
" fometimes debt and prifoners of war. Trials
" are fair and open except thofe for witchcraft,
" which are fecret. Other crimes are generally
" punifhed by flavery: but the principals in
" witchcraft are generally ftrangled and then
" burnt. The reft of the family are made
" flaves—never knew nor heard of kidnapping.

" †When in the king's floop, he often went
" into the country feveral days at a time and
" once croffed from *Senegal* to *Goree* by crof-
" fing in a ferry; always heard that on the coaft
" of *Senegal* particularly flaves were made for
" crimes; but moft of them came down the
" river from inland. Never heard of villages
" of that country being pillaged to procure
" flaves—certainly never heard of their being
" kid-

* Knox, N.º I. from page 19 to page 28.
† Mackintofh, N.º I. from page 28 to page 35.

" kidnapped by the natives—has heard of their
" being kidnapped by the Europeans; but no
" man ever told him he faw it—never faw it
" happen. In 1778 he was there, a fingle fhip,
" when the war had ftopped the flave-trade and
" he wifhed to reduce the price: he reafoned
" with them about the folly of keeping it up,
" when there was likely to be no buyer; afked
" a chief what he would do with his flaves then?
" obferving that he muft let them go again
" (meaning prifoners of war), the chief re-
" plied—' *What them go again to come to kill me*
" *again?*'—in fhort he gave me to underftand
" that they would put them to death."

The evidences of the *whole* of the *firft number*
run in parallel with thofe which I have quoted,
and the firft number comprifes more than *two
thirds* of the whole of the examinations of the
Committee of the Houfe of Commons upon *that
part* of the fubject which refers to the *coafts of
Africa.*

To counteract thefe evidences, *Captain Wilfon, Captain Hills, Mr. Wadftrom, Mr. How,* and
General Rooke, have given their *evidence.* Extracts from their evidence upon this bufinefs
Mr. Wilberforce has quoted, and which in his
fpeech have been circulated in *two penny pamphlets,* but none of thofe which I have *here*
quoted.

As to the whole of the evidence of *Mr. Clarkfon*—his is all hearfay—all at fecond hand—the

result of a misunderstanding betwixt *himself* and
Mr. Norris, who (as he says) gave him the information, and which is denied by *Mr. Norris.*
His evidence, therefore, upon the subject can,
in the fairnefs of justice, be only confidered as
that opinion which any other person might have
formed who has never been there ; provided alfo
his enthufiafm, like *Mr. Clarkfon's,* had fubjugated his reafon.

But neither *Captain Wilfon, Captain Hills,*
Mr. Wadftrom, Mr. How, or *General Rooke,*
go fo far as to contradict the general and principal caufes of the Africans being fold to flavery,
and as they are ftated by the evidences which I
have quoted. Thefe caufes, which exifted in the
beginning, exift now and perhaps ever will—
whether the Englifh interfere or not.

Thefe witnefles only affert that the *African*
flavery is increafed by the temptation of barter,
and I am not difpofed to difbelieve them, for
I wifh to follow the truth as far as I can trace
it—that kidnapping is dreaded and detefted,
and even punifhed when detected. Now if
that be the cafe—the very circumftance proves
the practice not to be general, and that it is not
affociated with the common and principal
caufes of *slavery* there. It appears that a fingle
negroe can by arming himfelf guard againft
the practice. I will put this queftion to thofe
who have read the whole of the evidence upon

I   the

the *African slavery*—Whether in their confci-
ences they do not know that if the European
fhips from every power trading there were withdrawn—the prifoners taken in war—the adulterers—the thieves and the debtors, would not
be put to death? I am of opinion that they
would—and the Houfe of Commons, by their
laft vote upon the queftion, confirms to me that
a large majority of rational men will always
think fo, and know fo too.

The teftimonies which I have quoted and
the remaining evidences of others fimilar to
them are not the *inventions* of the *prefent day,*
but are correfponding with and confirming that
original motive of *humanity* which firft encouraged Englifhmen to embark in the trade—to
fave the lives of thofe wretches who would be
otherwife devoted victims to the barbarous laws
of their native country—to refcue fuch by
barter from certain death, and to place them
where their lives thus forfeited may be yet preferved and made ufeful under the protection of
mafters practifed by education and natural pro-
penfity in acts of *humanity*.

The *captains* of *trading veffels* are much more
competent witneffes for clearing up that point
which is only neceffary to be afcertained becaufe
it will alone decide—*whether the trade be an act
of humanity or the very contrary.*

For

For if the *Africans* would be *put to death* if not taken away, *it is an act of humanity to receive them.* But if they are made *slaves* purely becaufe of the temptation which is offered of felling them to the *European traders,* it is then *an act of inhumanity* which *ought not* ever to be repeated.

The *trading captains* have without hefitation or one fingle contradiction proved the formei and the oppofite evidence does not go fo far as to deny it. The *trading captains* vifit and revifit the coaft; the oppofite witneffes have once touched upon it and never returned. The *trading captains* are not the merchants who receive the profits of the voyage: they conduct thofe fhips as they would fhips to other deftinations and are no more to be difcredited in their relations upon this point than others would be upon what paffed in the *Eaft* or *Weft-Indies*— in *New Zealand* or in *Greenland.*

The oppofite witneffes in their evidence do not contradict the fact that the African flaves *would be put to death if not taken away*; but they affert that *fome are made slaves* becaufe there is a market for the fale of them—that fome have been kidnapped from a *predilection for their perfons*—and morever, that the baneful effects of *intoxicating fpirits,* experienced long by the *Englifh,* have found their way to *Africans* and increafed their favage barbarities beyond that

I 2 degree

degree they would otherwife have extended. Their evidences do not contradict the prefent exiftence of the firft natural caufe, but they furnifh an undoubted proof of the pernicious *effects of fpirituous liquors* :—that whether the practice be indulged by a *barbarian* or a *chriftian* it extinguifhes every fpark of humanity in the heart.

Having ftated thus much, I fhall proceed to the examination of Mr. Wilberforce's *fpeech*, which is founded, as all our knowledge upon this queftion muft be, upon *the evidence before the Committee of the Houfe of Commons*, but it does not explain to any extent the *original nature* of the *Slave Trade*, nor prove from the evidence before him that which was moft devoutly wifhed to be inveftigated.

There was an obvious reafon for this, and I truft I fhall be able clearly to demonftrate it.

Had the whole of the truth been laid open and made known, men would have been no longer doubtful upon the queftion; and if the *firft caufe* of our trading there had been proved to be *ftill exifting*, Mr. Wilberforce was not fo weak in underftanding as not to be convinced in his own mind that it *pofitively has humanity for its bafis*.

Mr. W. fets out with the following promife of future fincerity—" that he wifhed to difcufs " the fubject frankly indeed but with fairnefs " and moderation. He trufted that the debate, " inftead

" inflead of exciting afperity and confirming
" prejudice, would tend to produce a general
" conviction of the truth of what in fact was
" incontrovertible—That the abolition of the
" Slave Trade was indifpenfably required of
" them, not only by religion and morality, but
" by every principle of found policy."

It might have been prefumed that Mr. Wilberforce from this declaration had been difpofed
to have evinced in his *fpeech* that open integrity
which he firft avowed, and to have commanded
a decifive tribute to *truth* and *juftice* by the
concurrence of the Houfe of Commons with
his *plain* and *open* opinion of the *African Slave
Trade* in its prefent ftate.

But that part of his fpeech was fo narrowed
and contracted—fo little calculated to illuftrate
the truth—that it only tended to conceal and
obfcure it. The truth and the whole of the
truth would not have anfwered his purpofe. He
moft certainly cannot be fuppofed to be ignorant
of the queftion—whether without thefe temptations which he has ftated being put into practice
there were befides *a great majority of slaves*
whom it would be *humanity* to receive on board.
I think he has clearly proved that he was aware
of the confequences of it upon the minds of the
houfe, and therefore with all his profeffed candour purpofely avoided the inveftigation.

An upright judge cloathed in the ermine of
juftice

juſtice would have dwelt upon the relative importance of every evidence and ſcrupulouſly
weighed the whole of the examinations. He
would have attached the greateſt confidence on
thoſe that appeared to be the moſt uniform and
explicit in their evidence—to thoſe who were
the moſt competent to give it in the moſt ample
manner for the purpoſe of a thorough information. But all ſuch Mr. Wilberforce has caſt
into the back ground—he has artfully turned
exceptions into general rules and *general rules*
into exceptions : he has degraded the evidence
of thoſe who were uniform in giving a full information upon the deſired queſtion and whoſe
information tended to prove—*that what had,
when formerly done, been humanity, was, ſo done,
now humanity.*

He has brought forward detached paſſages
ſelected from the evidence of viſitors upon the
coaſt, who knew nothing of the general cauſe
of their being *slaves* and being *ſold*, and whoſe
information at the moſt could extend no farther
than every *traveller* will ſuperficially acquire in
every country he goes to.

If in England a ſerjeant wants to decoy a
young man, he will firſt make him drunk—if in
England a ſhip's crew be wanted, the captain
will be armed with the power of preſs warrants.
If a *foreigner* ſaw theſe practices, he might upon
an examination prove them, but does it follow

from

from hence that every foldier and failor are thus kidnapped?

Without being reduced to the neceffity of urging fuch weak argument—without affigning fuch *remote* caufes for the production of *slaves*—caufes more *proximate* and natural will readily occur to thofe who *aim* to inform themfelves of the truth. And if caufes fimilar prevail in *chriftian* countries, where the paffions are difciplined by *religion* as well as *law*, there will be lefs difficulty in fuppofing more natural caufes for the forfeiture of freedom and life amongft a *favage race* of *barbarians*.

If *Britain* configns *her felons* to *slavery* whom fhe fpares from the gallows—if prifoners taken in war be *retained* for *ranfom, fupport*, or *reciprocal exchange*—if *adulterers* would be imprifoned for ever if they could *not* pay the fine—if fuch abide the punifhment of *our* laws—the *Africans* only do the fame in a *ruder form*. They have no *fhipping* to entertain their outcafts, and no power to command a *fettlement* far beyond the confines of their coafts :—they therefore *would* deftroy them if not tempted to mercy by the alternative of *barter*.

Do the evidences recited by Mr. Wilberforce contradict thefe facts, or does Mr. Wilberforce ftate them?—certainly neither. He knew too well that fuch were not calculated to catch the *greedy ears of thofe who devour up his difcourfe*—

not

not calculated for the *methodijt preachers—for*
the falfe ideas of humanity in a *Sharpe* or a
Clarkfon—nor for roufing the attention of fleep-
ing philofophy in its elbow chair at *Oxford* or
Cambridge.

I fhall conclude this part of the fubject very
different from the manner of Mr. Wilberforce,
who, after he has felected the inflammatory
fcraps—expatiated upon them—and turned the
only fubftantial evidence into infignificance—af-
fumes a tone of horrow to cover the unfairnefs
of his own arrangement.

I entreat *fellow citizens* to confider the whole
of the evidence upon the *African Slave Trade*—
then to examine their own hearts after they
have acquired the neceffary information—whether it would not be an *act of humanity* to receive
on board our fhips thofe devoted to death inftead of abandoning them to their fate—and
to be perfuaded before they yield, that as this
was the indifputable principle which *firft*
prompted the Legiflature to adopt the trade,
fo fhould it not be difcontinued without a thorough conviction that when it ceafes *the caufe of
humanity is ferved.*

No one will be fo hardy as to fay that we
fhould renounce that which *humanity* charges
us to continue, becaufe unfounded fufpicion
has ftirred up an alarm:—it is a very ftrong reafon why we fhould aim to make a more nice
diftinction

diſtinction by thoroughly informing the under-
ſtanding.

We are not reſponſible for the paſſions and
the vices of Africans—we are only reſponſible
for *our own* conduct. If we anchor on their
coaſts and offer no direct or indirect temptations—
—if *ſlaves* are brought for us to receive on
board, which would otherwiſe be *put to death*—
we are acting yet *in the cauſe of humanity.*

I have not availed myſelf of that argument
which I have often heard from the tongues of
others—that if we abandon the *African trade*
it will ſtill be continued by the *French*, the
Dutch, the *Spaniards*, and the *Danes.* It is not
that ſort of argument which will operate in my
breaſt for the cauſe of humanity.

If I thought this cauſe a bad one, I ſhould
not wait for an example from others to teach
me to deſert it—and when I did deſert it—it
ſhould be alone from the *conviction of reaſon.*

From the moment of time that the *African
ſlaves* are received on board an Engliſh veſſel
and which *ſlaves* have not been decoyed by any
act of the Engliſh on board—from that moment of time, I look upon it, that the reſponſibility of this country in behalf of the captives.
commences ; and at the moment of time that
theſe captives are *delivered over* to the *planters* in
the *Weſt-India iſlands*, then and not till then,
their reſponſibility commences.

K

I con-

I confider the caufe of the trade as directly originating with this country—it being carried on by the merchants—the fhipping—the failors of England—and under the fanction of Englifh laws. It is our part therefore to regulate what is termed the *Middle Paffage.* It is for our Houfe of Commons to judge of their own acts — to provide fhips that are fitting, and captains that are humane. In all tranfactions confidence muft have a neceffary fhare ; and I fee no reafon why the humanity of an Englifh Captain, becaufe he commands a fhip bound to the *African coaft*, fhould be fufpected or marked with particular obloquy.

I therefore fhall not purfue Mr. Wilberforce's fpeech through the Middle Paffage—but on his *arrival* at the *Weft-Indies* I fhall meet him *there* ; where I prefume I fhall be capable of judging upon the fubject at leaft as well as he— of fpeaking upon it not as an *ear witnefs* but an *eye witnefs.*

At any rate I will not conceal the truth to promote a weak caufe—I will not be fufpected of *hypocrify* by felecting only fuch evidence as tends to ferve the purpofe of *enthufiafm*, but not the caufe of *reafon* and *truth*—my comments fhall be formed by their ftandard alone. If I promife much, be it remembered that Mr. Wilberforce promifed more.

On the Condition of Slaves in the Weſt-India Iſlands.

As the principal topick which urged the Debates in the Houſe of Commons for *two* ſucceſſive days in April 1791 was on a motion for the *abolition of the Slave Trade*, he who for information adverted to it would have been led to ſuppoſe that ſuch an important queſtion would have been debated in a manner *ſo open*—that the true nature of the origin and continuance of that trade would have been plainly aſcertained—that the light of truth let in upon it would have been as broad as that from the ſhining ſun at noon day.

But I appeal to any man who has read theſe Debates, and who has not read the *Examinations* upon which they ought to have been founded, whether he can from them alone, draw this plain inference—*that the Slave Trade ought upon principle in humanity to be aboliſhed.*

I will anſwer for it that *every part* of Mr. Wilberforce's *ſpeech* was printed with the moſt anxious ſedulity, and that what his art did not inſtruct him to conceal, the pens of *enthuſiaſts* did not heſitate to ſet down—and I am certain

K 2

that

that conviction upon principle is not to be found there.

No fpeaker on that fide of the queftion—and that fide by far embraced the moft powerful—dwelt with any energy or with any pretence of convincing the underftanding, on the *neceffity* in *humanity* for the *abolition of the Slave Trade* : and this was the reafon—*becaufe from the whole of the argument upon the whole of the evidence, the trade would have been proved to be founded in humanity.*

The Houfe of Commons in order to have come to a right underftanding ought to have made the *African Queftion* a *diftinct* one from that of the Middle Paffage, and the conditions of negroes in the Weft-India iflands ; and then it would have appeared evident to reafon that in their proceedings they were carrying along with them truth for their juftification : for in my opinion the afcertaining beyond a doubt whether it be an *act of humanity or not* to continue on the *African Slave Trade*, forms the key-ftone of the whole of the queftion.

For if the Houfe of Commons were ever to refolve that Englifh veffels fhall no longer import into Englifh colonies *flaves* of other nations —and if that refolution be founded, upon the abftract principle, that the *hearts of Britifh Senators revolt at the idea of flavery*, it will be exacted from them that their conduct be uniform—

form—and then it will be apparent that they cannot refolve upon fuch a principle in *Africa* and negative it in the *West-India islands.*

If freedom be the univerfal theme—if that be the object—if they will not receive the *Africans* into *flavery* whom they *have not* in their power—they muft, to be uniform, reftore to freedom the *flaves* that they *have* in their power.

But this fort of argument is not fuited to the *trimming* or *accommodating* humanity of Mr. Wilberforce, nor is it found congenial to thofe who have addreffed upon the fubject or preached upon it at *methodift meetings.* They do not come prepared in their arguments to pay the price for univerfal freedom—*firft* to purchafe the liberty of the negroes in the Weft-Indies, and *then* to find a refource among themfelves for fupplying two millions of annual deficiency in the revenue. No, fay they—*abolish* the importation of *flaves*, and *regulate thofe* imported. Let the latter ftill be *flaves*—There is a thing called " *State neceffity*" that controuls the liberal fuffufions of their hearts, and that tells them, that fo far they fhall go and no farther.

Even *he* who has been long accuftomed to lead and not to follow, becaufe *he* poffeffes the foundeft underftanding and the warmeft heart— even *Mr. Fox* has been obliged to limit his natural outlines of freedom in order to entertain

that

that *accommodating* humanity of Mr. Wilberforce.   The *eagle* has defcended to the haunt of
the *humming bird*.

For when Mr. Wilberforce, five years ago,
firft fpoke of the *abolition of the Slave Trade*, it
was then that *Mr. Fox* fpoke out like a man who
views every fubject with an enlarged fight.
" Let," fays he, " not only the *Slave Trade*
be *abolifhed*, but let the *negroes in the Weft-Indies
be free*."—But thefe were only the fentiments of
a great philanthropift in the abftract.—Mr. *Fox*
at that moment had not annexed to them a
country entangled by a national debt, and driven
to the loweft means for raifing a revenue.   As
foon as he did, *State neceffity* moderated his ar-
dor, and that natural idea of unbounded freedom has never fince been reverberated within
the walls of the *Senate*—not once during the
two long days debate.

When I compare thefe high-founding decla-
mations for freedom in theory with that which
from *State neceffity* can only be in practice—
when I reflect on the little power we have left
for the exertion of humanity whilft thus op-
preffed by the prefent load of taxes—when I
am told of the profperity of this country, whilft
the taxes which contribute to pay off the annual
fcore are drawn in a great meafure from the
promotion of *vice*—I can then take upon me to
fay,

say, that whatever might be the *inclinations* of the hearts of Englishmen, they at this moment of time have no more freedom, humanity, or wealth than they themselves have a pressing occasion for.—The *Lilliputs* of *Gulliver* can do as much.

It is high time for us to be told that these generous sacrifices to freedom are now *beyond* our power—that there is an ample scope for more wealth and humanity than we possess in the contemplation of reform *at home*—that a melioration of the conditions of the lower class of people and a correction of their *vices* are expected from our nature, justice and humanity.

I will be bound for it that the *West-India planters* will discharge *their duty* towards *their poor* without being *insulted* into it by us. But if they stood in need of the inquisitorial eye of this country—it would be directed towards them upon an honester principle and with better effect, when we proved to them by *example*, what we now only exact by *precept*.

Is it not of some consideration for the *West-India planters* to know whether the *Slave Trade* is to be *abolished or not?* and do not the regulations of those under their protection depend in a great measure upon it? For more than five years they have been kept in suspense—have been unable to embark in new undertakings—to clear away fresh lands, or, from the *shock of credit,*

credit, to purchase such as have lately been offered for sale.

Ought not the question to have been dropped before now ? or is it that question which is purposely defigned for ever to attract the attention of the people of this country ? left, whenever it be withdrawn—they will find themselves at leisure, and their minds will be abruptly occupied (as if they had never seen the *fight* before) with the hard conditions of their *own poor.*

After the witnesses were all examined—after the House of Commons was furnished with all the information that was deemed to be satisfactory—and after the long debate of *two* successive days, why was not the consequent Division the final agitation of the subject ?

Were not four years an ample space of time for the investigation ?—or did not the opponents of the *African Slave Trade* make the *most* of that long opportunity, and are now repairing that neglect by invigorating their system *afresh ?* —by alarming the minds of the *credulous*—by circulating with *fresh* industry partial *inflammatory extracts* in *twopenny* pamphlets through all parts of the kingdom ?

Is the imaginary cruelty of the *West-India planters* to be the theme of every *drinking club* and *psalm singing meeting?* and are *they* to submit to have their names branded with acts of barbarity for ever ? But I trust that, in the event,

event, men will not be thus cheated of their reafon.—I truft that as the fubject is to come again into the Houfe of Commons, the *African Queftion* will be *more homely* inveftigated, and the intention which induced Mr. Wilberforce to keep back the truth will be *fully detected*—I truft that thofe who voted in fupport of the *African Trade* will take care that the publick fhall fully underftand it; and when they do, I have not much to fear from their juftice.

Before I proceed to remark upon Mr. Wilberforce's fpeech, I wifh to imprefs fome facts upon the minds of my readers.—

That the *Abridgement* of the Minutes of the *Evidence* taken before a *Committee* of the whole Houfe of Commons to whom it was referred to confider of the *Slave Trade* was printed in four numbers for the ufe of the Members *only*, and that they contain in the whole 650 *pages* in octavo.

Thefe four numbers are filled up with the whole of that evidence upon which the Debate of *two* days, in *April* 1791, was fupported ; and when Mr. Wilberforce in his *fpeech* gave, *Extracts* of *Evidence*, he felected them out of one or other of thefe *four numbers.*

In that part of his *fpeech* which relates to the evidence on the conditions of negroes in the *Weft-India Iflands*, he has ftudioufly betrayed the fame partiality by his choice of inflammatory

L   and

and paffionate paffages, that he did in his *brief* narrative of the tranfactions on the *African coaft*— and he has throughout the whole of it evidently evinced, that if he was adequate to the tafk of treating the fubject with reafon and candour, he was neither difpofed by temper or inclination to fulfil it.

But there is one point that I muft not omit becaufe it ftrongly confirms the truth of my argument and alfo the notoriety of Mr. Wilberforce's partiality.—It fhews what a man will do— what lengths he will go—and what little credit ought to be given to that *reafon* which is fubjugated by the overbearing dominion of *prejudice.*

When Mr. Wilberforce was debating the Queftion of *African Slavery,* he quoted paffages from the evidence of *vifitors* to that coaft, and affirmed that they ought to be credited in preference to the captains of the trading veffels. I, in anfwer to that, have faid—that thofe who were the moft converfant in the fubject, are ever the moft capable of paffing a right opinion. If the *captains* had given the moft favourable evidences for his purpofe, he would have found it convenient to have reverfed his argument, for he has done fo in the fubfequent part of his fpeech upon the condition of the *negroes in the Weft-India Iflands,* and which I fhall fhortly prove.

I, for my part, do not lay any ftrefs upon the evidence

evidence of *vifitors* neither on the coafts *of Africa* nor *in the Weft-Indies*; I only make the remark as a comment upon Mr. Wilberforce's profeffions of juftice, candour and humanity. *Vifitors* are not competent evidence for the whole truth at either place, and they never meant to take upon them that ability. It is Mr. Wilberforce who has taken that liberty with their names for ferving his own purpofe in argument.

But the obfervations which I have already made will furnifh my readers with a reafon, why Mr. Wilberforce quoted the names of *vifitors* as the *beft* evidence on the *African coaft* becaufe it made for his caufe, and why he omitted the evidence of *vifitors* to the *Weft-Indies* becaufe it made againft his caufe. *Admirals Shul-dam, Barrington, Arbuthnot, Edwards, Hotham, Captain Lambert, Commodore Gardner, Lord Macartney, Sir John Dalling,* and *Lord Rodney,* all have given an unequivocal evidence of the humanity *of the Weft-India planters* towards their negroes. Of all thefe names Mr. Wilberforce has not dropped a *fingle tittle.* This was necef-fary to be known, becaufe his *fpeech* is circula-ted every where, and the cruelties recorded in it are become as familiar to *children* as the ftory of *Blue Beard* or *Jack the Giant killer.*

I will take upon me to fay, that I have, no more than the gentlemen above quoted, feen during three years practice of phyfick in the

Weft-

Weft-India iflands any other treatment than that which humanity dictates. I will go further—that during my practice I never was called to give *furgical relief* to any negroe who had fuffered from the feverity of chaftifement.

If I were difpofed to feaft with a rancorous rapture on the fordid catalogue of cruelties perpetrated in *England*, I would be bound to collect a blacker lift in feven days, than could be found in all the *Weft-India iflands* in as many years. The whole of their miferies may be detected almoft at one view—one is not obliged to fearch for them in *jails*, and in *garrats*, in *houfes of correction*, and upon *dunghills*. When the lift is read over, after the gang is drawn out, thofe that are abfent are readily to be reforted to. This is that Mr. Wilberforce who firft fets out with befpeaking the difpofition of the Houfe of Commons to *candour!*

I will now felect fome paffages from the moft competent evidences on the *conditions* of *negroes* in the *Weft-India Iflands*; but I do not felect them for the purpofe of exacting that my readers fhall depend upon thefe alone for furnifhing their reafon with the true nature of the queftion—that can only be obtained by reading the *whole* of the evidence. *Thefe quotations* will fhew what the nature of that evidence is which Mr. Wilberforce has chofen to reject—*they* are given as *famples* of what are remaining behind.

My

My only motive is to affure my countrymen that whatever prejudices they have formed are owing to their having been grofsly impofed upon—and that thofe who doubt will have their doubts removed, by examining the *four numbers* to which I have referred them—and it muft not be forgotten, that it was by that reference alone, the Houfe of Commons, in fpite of Mr. Wilberforce's pitiable pleadings, faw the queftion in the light that they did, and voted *accordingly*.

Gilbert Franklyn, Esq. a native of England, refided in theWeft-Indies 21 years. He has depofed, " That managers kind behaviour to his
" negroes, fo as to gain their affections while he
" makes them do their bufinefs, is to him, and
" he believes to moft people, a higher recom-
" mendation than his fkill as a planter. One
" of the firft things enquired into, is his cha-
" racter in that refpect ; no perfon would em-
" ploy a manager of a cruel character, believing
" him to be fuch. Such treatment is fcarcely
" poffible to be practifed in fecrefy.

" He does not believe the poor in any country
" live happier than the negroes on plantations
" in the Weft-India Iflands; in many cafes
" they have an evident fuperiority: their la-
" bour is flight, good care is taken of them
" in ficknefs and in health, and they have no
" occafion to fear the diftreffes of their chil-
" dren from inability to labour. He thinks
" their

" their lot in general is to be envied by the
" poor of all countries he has seen.

" Negroes generally conceal their money,
" and do not chuse to be thought rich. He
" had himself a negroe who bought out the
" freedom of his wife at the price of 8ol. and
" poffeffed two houfes. He believes he was
" worth 6 or 700l.—he afked for his freedom,
" and obtained it from the witnefs, who en-
" deavoured to diffuade him from the requeft.
" There is reafon to believe he has fince loft
" one third of what he was worth. Many of
" the negroes poffefs a great deal of property."
His evidence extends from page 28 to page 41
in No. II. of the Abridgment of Evidence, &c.

Sir Afhton Warner Byam, his Majefty's At-
torney General for Grenada, lived on various
iflands from 1765 to 1789—owns no land, but
an uncleared tract, and never intends to fettle;
he has depofed, "That in Grenada a flave is tria-
" ble before one magiftrate for fmall offences;
" for capital crimes before two or more, one
" being of the quorum. Since he left the ifland
" he underftands a law has paffed, taken from
" the Antigua practice, by which three or more
" freeholders are to be called in by the magif-
" trates as jurors or affeffors. Compared with
" the punifhments in England on the fame
" offences, he thinks the criminal laws far from
" fevere—whipping and confinement are the
                                        " only

" only punishments by the master or manager,
" which are confidered as legal. The quantity
" of punishment will undoubtedly vary with
" the master's difpofition; but any abufe of the
" master's power was always confidered pu-
" nishable by indictment or information. If
" fuch abufe was frequent, he never knew it;
" and confidering the nature of the master's
" power, and the variety of the perfons who
" may acquire it, he has always thought abufes
" of it not more frequent than fimilar abufes of
" power in England. In general thinks the
" Weft-India laws fufficient to protect flaves in
" life and limb.

" When he was Solicitor General in 1775 or
" 1776, a white man was executed for the
" murder of his flave. A flave's comfort de-
" pends as much on his master's temper, as
" that of the English apprentice does on his
" master's; believes no one has doubted that a
" criminal would fuffer for the murder of a
" flave exactly as for that of a free perfon.

" On all eftates flaves were at the field work
" by day break, but nurfing women had always
" an hour or an hour and half beyond that time,
" with half an hour at breakfaft, and two hours
" reft in their houfes at noon; they wrought
" till the clofe of the day; they then threw
" grafs to the ftock, and went home for the
" night. In crop they work later, and on fome
" eftates

" eftates the work there goes on all night and
" day, by fpells, both of white fervants and'
" flaves. It is univerfally remarked, that the
" negroes in crop are the moft healthy and
" cheerful.

" By the late Grenada act, planters are
" obliged to allot land to their flaves, and
" *guardians* are appointed to infpect each
" eftate's provifion ground.

" Saturday afternoon out of crop, and all
" Sunday the whole year, were very generally
" allowed for working fuch grounds; and he
" thinks the faid act has fixed it from twelve
" o'clock on Saturday. This time is fufficient
" not only for raifing the neceffary food, but
" alfo for the flave's carrying to market his fur-
" plus provifions and his poultry, &c.

" Negroes have ufually furplus produce, ex-
" cept perhaps a very few idle ones, probably
" in all gangs. He has known many flaves buy
" their freedom. Believes the king's fhips,
" and merchantmen, are chiefly fupplied with
" vegetables, poultry, &c. by negroes on their
" own account.

" Every eftate has an hofpital. A furgeon
" vifits the flaves twice a week, or oftener if
" required. One or more nurfes attend the
" fick. The owner provides wine and other
" comforts recommended by the furgeon."

As

As far as my memory is impreſſed with tranſactions in the Weſt-Indies ſo remote as 20 years ago, I can take upon me to ſay, that every extract out of the evidence of the above witneſs, is an interruption of that general purity and accordance, which pervade every part of it. It conveys in the moſt conciſe manner every circumſtance that tends to ſhew the general ſtate of the negroes, and of the laws in the Weſt-India iſlands. It is delivered with candour and moderation, and moreover with the ſtricteſt regard to the cauſe of truth and humanity. His evidence follows that of Mr. *Franklyn's* and extends from page 41 to 54 in No. II.

Alexander Campbell, Eſq. reſided in the Weſt-Indies from 1754 to 1788. He gives an accurate evidence of the whole of the duties of a planter, of the buſineſs of planters, of the conditions of the negroes, and of the nature of the climate and the produce. His evidence extends from page 55 to page 74 in No. II.

" The Grenada Legiſlature paſſed a law for
" inſpecting negroe grounds, in 1766, and
" another in 1788. Negroes may raiſe poul-
" try and hogs, and ſell them for the beſt price
" they can get—they are forced to labour at
" their own ground.

" They raiſe, for their own uſe, or for ſale in
" Grenada and the ceded iſlands, plantanes and

M " fig-

" fig-bananas, caſſada, yams, &c. and alſo
" cabbages, ſhallots, &c. likewiſe pine apples,
" water melons, &c. Every one of theſe the
" negroes have in their grounds at ſome time
" or other of the year.

    " New negroes are cloathed and placed with
" the chief negroes, and regularly fed thrice a
" day, for a year or more, till they have enough
" food on their grounds. They generally are
" allowed to ſell the firſt proviſion they raiſe to
" attach them to the eſtate and encourage them.
" Property they can call their own makes them
" happy, and gives them a better idea of their
" ſtate. Maſters very often give them poul-
" try, and encourage them to rear them.

    " In general, the negroes ſell proviſions,
" poultry, and hogs. A ſlave who makes pro-
" per uſe of his time may ſell produce to the
" value of from 7l. to 15l. ſterling yearly.
" Some induſtrious negroes, who have good
" land, often ſell from 30l. to 40l. ſterling.
" Slaves with children have a greater propor-
" tion of land than ſingle ſlaves, and he believes
" in the ceded iſlands half the current ſpecie is
" the property of the negroes.

    " Knows no where a greater proportion of
" able experienced medical men than in the
" Weſt-Indies. There are about forty in Gre-
" nada, where they are allowed 7s 6d currency
" for each ſlave young and old, and paid be-
                                    " ſides

" fides for fractures and operations, and 20s
" currency per head for inoculation.

" Plantation punifhment is not fo fevere as
" fifty lafhes given to a foldier, and is foon
" cured. Great crimes are often forgiven to
" negroes who have not been punifhed before,
" becaufe, after feveral floggings, they confider
" it as little punifhment. Good negroes feel
" the difgrace more than the whipping. In ten
" years, ending 1788, he faw no beggars or mi-
" ferable objects except at Barbadoes, where he
" faw many whites of that defcription, fome
" ferving free negroes and flaves, who pay a
" weekly fum to their mafters.

" All the new negroes he bought feemed to
" be in a favage ftate. Thofe of the gold coaft
" appeared more tractable and induftrious. They
" generally fhewed themfelves off to be bought,
" and when examined feemed difappointed if
" refufed. On feeing their countrymen on the
" eftates, cloathed and comfortable, they feemed
" very happy. He knows not that he ever faw
" one otherwife. He has often afked fome of
" his flaves, if they wifhed to return to Africa,
" and their univerfal anfwer was, ' no mafter,
" me know better.' They wifh not to be thought
" Africans, and with them ' falt water negree'
" and ' favage' have the fame meaning.

" Thinks, if the fexes were equalifed by buy-
" ing

" ing more women, it would ftill be impoffible
" for the flaves to be kept up by breeding.

" He never knew but one man in Grenada,
" who was faid to ufe his flaves more fevere
" than common, but what his property was
" ruined. Thinks flaves are treated much bet-
" ter than when he firft knew the Weft-Indies.

" Domeftick and field flaves are generally
" healthy; if any thing the former die fafter
" than the latter, owing probably to their ram-
" bling more at nights, efpecially the young
" men.

" In all the Englifh and French iflands, he
" knows free negroes and Mulattoes are confi-
" dered as a nuifance, as they never cultivate
" lands themfelves, and the women huxter pro-
" vifions, fell rum, and receive ftolen goods,
" corrupting the flaves morals.

" In Grenada, all the Creoles and moft new
" negroes are Chriftians, being generally chrif-
" tened two or three years after their arrival.
" They often read the fervice over the dead.
" They often attend the churches, Englifh and
" Catholick. The clergy by law muft chriften
" them gratis, and certain times yearly vifit and
" inftruct them. Believes the negroes in the
" other ceded iflands are equally religious,
" though there is no fuch law.

" Negroes are naturally fond of gay drefs, and
" though allowed fufficient working day cloaths
" they

" they buy fine cloaths for Sundays. It is
" very common in Grenada and the ceded
" iflands to fee field negroes in white dimity
" jackets and breeches and fine Holland fhirts;
" and the women in muflins, and four or fiveIndia
" muflin handkerchiefs on their heads at eight
" òr ten fhillings each. He has often feen
" flaves give feafts to 100 or 200 other flaves,
" with every rarity of the ifland and wines,
" which he could not have given for 6ol. fter-
" ling, and they very often borrow their mafter's
" plate and linen to entertain their friends.
" Thefe feafts are very frequent amongft the
" flaves. When large hogs are killed by the
" plantation negroes, they are commonly fold
" to the reft in fmall quantities.

" In Grenada the negroes go to their ground
" at 9 o'clock on Sunday morning and return
" about 12. They then drefs, and dance or
" walk till about 7 o'clock, when they affemble
" to prayers which they never neglect. After
" prayers they pafs the reft of the evening in
" their houfes."

James Baillie Efq. refident in the Weft-Indies
about 16 years. His evidence extends from
page 74 to page 80 in No. II.

" Would not have purchafed had he concei-
" ved Great Britain would have prohibited the
" importation of African negroes.

" Punifh-

" Punifhments not fevere when compared
" with the difcipline of the army and navy.

" Greateft attention is ufed to prevent the
" feparation of flaves connected either by rela-
" tionfhip or friendfhip. Never knew flaves
" exprefs a defire to return home. Slaves in
" Grenada are generally Chriftians in a ftate of
" comfort and happinefs.

" Recollects negroe freemen marrying flaves,
" though they know the children of fuch mar-
" riages will be born flaves.

" Introduction of new flaves cannot be pre-
" vented by any regulation of this country.

" Plough cannot be ufed.

" Lands cannot be cultivated by Europeans.

" Never was in Africa and therefore cannot
" fay whether the negroes imported from Africa
" are taken from a more happy ftate to be
" placed in a worfe; but believes, from infor-
" mation, that they are more comfortable in the
" Weft-Indies than in their own country.

" Provifions in the ifland are of quick growth."

Mr. Robert Thomas refided about 9 years in
St. Kitts and Nevis, as a Surgeon, and attended between 4000 and 5000 negroes annually
His evidence extends from page 85 to page 91
in No. II.

" Had every opportunity of obferving how
" negroes were treated, worked, fed, lodged,
" andcloathed.

" Has

" Has positive evidence that the slaves in the
" West-Indies, have a decided superiority, as
" to every comfort of life, over the common
" labourers and poor people of Ireland and
" Scotland; by being regularly supplied with
" every necessary of life, cloathing, food, com-
" fortable house, protection in health, the best
" advice in sickness, and on their decease, hav-
" ing a father and protector for their children."

James Tobin, Esq. has lived ten or twelve
years in the West-Indies at different times,
chiefly in Nevis. Has often been at St. Kitts.
His evidence extends from page 92 to page 104
in No. II.

" On all estates there are regular sick nurses,
" and generally a surgeon employed by the
" year.

" Sick slaves have sago, portable soup, wine,
" fresh meat, &c. Poultry and mutton are
" often killed to make them broth. He knew
" a convalescent negroe slave have 16 lambs,
" each worth two dollars, killed for his use.

" Lame, incurably diseased, and aged ne-
" groes, have the same food, cloathing, and
" accommodation, as if perfectly serviceable.
" He is warranted to say, that the punishments
" of slaves are mild, compared to those of Bri-
" tish sailors and soldiers.

" Has great reason to think that the agitation
" of the question for abolishing the Slave Trade
" has

" has had effects on the West-India credit very
" baneful and extenfive.

" Has found it eafy to perfuade fome negroes
" to adopt fuch alterations in managing their
" affairs as might tend to their advantage; but
" in general, they are obftinately wedded to
" their own cuftoms.

" A fum fufficient to buy a field negroe's
" freedom, would not be a confiderable pro-
" perty in Nevis, if he chofe to fave the money
" he could earn inftead of fpending it in fineries
" for himfelf and his wives, and other fuper-
" fluities.

" His property depends chiefly on the quan-
" tity *and ftock of poultry he may raife.*"

It might be obferved, by a reference to the
pages, that I have felected the quotations from
every fucceeding witnefs—that I have not turned
to the right or the left from one number to another for them, but have gone on in the ftrait
line—in fuch a one as he who is *defirous* to explain the *truth* will ever purfue.

Almoft the *whole* of the evidence in the *four
numbers* are tending to confirm this fact—that in
no country *the poor* are fo comfortable as the
negroes in the *Weft-India islands.* This is the
general tenor of the evidence; and whatever
deviation is found, muft be confidered by rational men in its true fenfe, as an *exception* to a
general rule.

If

If I were to affert in evidence, becaufe the
ftreets in *London* fwarm with *beggars* and the
tongues of the intoxicated vulgar utter *blaf-
phemy*—becaufe *thoufands* are imprifoned and
thoufands ftarve—becaufe refractory work-
men who combine are dragged away to a
prifon, handcuffed, and guarded by the mili-
tary, and their families left to fhift for themfelves—ought it to be inferred from thefe facts,
that there is no provifion for the *poor*—no virtue
—no religion—no freedom *in England*?

I am proud to fay, for the caufe of humanity
and juftice, that the truth of the treatment of
negroes and *their children* is uniform with fuch
evidence as I have quoted, and not with that
which is felected from the *fpeech* of Mr. Wilberforce—and I am as much convinced as I ever
was of any one event yet in the womb of time,
that the more this queftion be inveftigated the
fooner the defign of Mr Wilberforce will be
detected and reviled.

He has attempted to impofe in his *fpeech*
upon human underftanding, and to miflead the
humanity of the country. Of every virtuous
act of the *Weft-Indian* his tongue is palfied in
the praife.

The time will come, and I truft it will not be
long firft, when the *Weft-India planter* will be
feen in that amiable view which he merits
for his humanity—*that humanity* which he has

N   the

the ampleft field for difplaying—and when the *condition* of the families under his protection will be the envy and not the pity of the miferably poor, and fettered prifoners of this country.

The Weft-Indian has the power of humanity in the fulleft extent; and it flows from him in that channel which our *firft nature* ordained.   It bleffes him who beftows it—for the kinder he is to his negroes, the more he is enriched.   It is to him like an inexhauftable fountain upon the fummit of a hill fupplied by the dews from heaven to water the vallies below—it is the oil in the widow's cruife that never will be dry— whereas the humanity of thofe in this country who feel for the mifreprefented *condition* of *negroes* can never be true—it can never extend to more than *falfe pity*. The *enthufiafts* have no more to give to the comfort of negroes than their *enthufiafm*—than their *pity*—which they miftake for *humanity*.

I will prefent the enthufiaft with a diftinction betwixt his *pity* and the *humanity* of the *Weft-Indian*—by the ftatement of a fair allufion : if I faw a perfon dying, and who was agonifed by pain, and the nature of whofe cafe was fuch that my art could not remedy, all that I had to beftow upon him would be the figh of *pity :* if I faw another perfon agonifed by pain, and the nature of whofe cafe was by my art curable, my *humanity* would be called upon, and by the judicious adminiftration of it, I fhould prove that I had

not

not the lefs remaining by having beftowed all that
was neceffary. Where the power of *humanity*
ceafes, *pity* commences. *Humanity* implies the
power of doing good, *pity* implies the defire
without the power. If a man of *humanity* fees
a beggar that he thinks is an object for *humanity*
he beftows him the boon. If one beggar meets
another they can only exchange their *pity*. It
is time for *Enthufiafts* to be told *what is their
power.*

The active perfeverance of Mr Wilberforce, in
his purfuit of this fubject, and in his keeping the
inveftigation alive in order to procure new information, and thereby to infufe additional conviction into the minds of the Houfe of Commons,
is all an *idle pretence.*

He has ranfacked already the country for characters fuited to his caufe, and who might truly
fay, like *Roderigo* in the *Play* of *Othello*—" I do
" follow in the chace, not like a hound that hunts,
" but one that fills up the cry. I think that the
" iffue will be, I fhall have fo much experience
" for my pains ; and fo with no money and a
" little more wit, return again *(not to the Weft-*
" *Indies)* to Venice."

No one will hereafter fay that this fubject had
not as folemn and deliberate an adjudication
when it was brought to a decifion in the Houfe
of Commons *in April* 1791 as any fubject that
ever came before the *Britifh Senate;* but Mr.
Wilberforce

Wilberforce aims to perfuade his followers in the chace that the motion was negatived—but the caufe of humanity *not defeated* : he takes a *frefh* date from that day, which in fairnefs of things, and for the fake of peace, ought to have been the *final* day : and from *that* date he invigorates *anew*, and revives with frefh afperity the *dying* caufe.

The minds of the credulous are to be frefh and frefh poifoned by printing his inflammatory quotations and by fuppreffing the evidence which is oppofed to them. His *fpeech* has found its way every where—has brought forward *frefh affociations, frefh petitions, frefh pamphlets*—has fo operated upon the actions of weak men, that it is almoft infanity to hope at converting them —whilft, in the mean while, the truth of the quef-tion, which led the Houfe of Commons to *their* decifion, is left out of thefe pamphlets—is funk and become unprofitable.

Mr. Wilberforce, like *Fame* defcribed in *Virgil*

> Parva primo metu mox fefe attollit in auras
> Ingrediturque folo—

grown every day bolder and bolder, from a pigmie to a giant—and attended by an hoft, marches in *front* with a *drawn fabre* in one hand and his *flaming fpeech* in the other, determined to cry havock and let loofe the dogs of war amongft the *negroes* againft their *mafters*, for deeds

of

of inhumanity falsely afferted and fouly per-fifted in. But as he brings this fubject forward again, he has judged right in being fo fpeedy, left the fountain be drained dry from whence he draws his fupport—left thofe who have hitherto pinned their credulity on his fleeve, fhould have feen the light of reafon, and difcovered *that truth,* he has aimed to conceal and wilfully pervert. The more this caufe be thoroughly fearched, the lefs *fupport* he will meet in the Houfe of Commons. A *fecond victory there* will be that of *truth* over *hypocrify.*

Neverthelefs, as *the Slave Trade to Africa* was originally an act of the *British* Senate, and as now the power of abolifhing or continuing it is totally with *them*—as fufpenfe has fo long waited or a threatened appeal *again* to their juftice—as Mr. Wilberforce is not to be rated in his conduct by the *ordinary ftandard* of reafon—it becomes a defenfive duty in the *Weft-India planters* to be alert in adopting the moft effectual means of *increafing* the population of *negroes* in the *Weft-India iflands.*

For without an additional fupply, or increafe of population, I am confident that all future frefh cultivations muft be deferred. It will be as much as the *planters can* hope, and more perhaps than they ever *can* do, to cultivate what they have already undertaken.

That

That they have fallen upon many methods of *increasing* the population of negroes I am well aware; and I am also perfuaded that no country abounds with men who poffefs more amply the means—who have more enlarged ideas of right and wrong—who have had more liberal educations—who have acquired more valuable knowledge—and who have warmer hearts, and more abounding with thofe generous qualities endowed to men in their *firft nature*—than the *Weft-India planters*.   There are also with them many *medical* men, who are ornaments to their profeffion.   With fuch a combination of power and *inclination*, it would be almoft a *folecifm* to fuppofe, that every means *have* not and *will* not be attempted for promoting that increafe of population among the negroes, fo devoutly to be wifhed.

My opinion of the *ftate* of the *negroes* in the *Weft-Indies exactly* accords with thofe delivered by *Mr. Thomas*, whom I have quoted, and *Dr. Samuel Athill*; they have refrefhed my recollection with the truth of thofe *original* impreffions left upon my mind when I left *the country in* 1769. I therefore fhall fpare a repetition of that which has been fo *fairly* given in their teftimonies.   But as there are fome points which I have reafoned with myfelf upon, and which have met with fome *approbation* when I have communicated them to others—I fhall beg to be indulged

dulged with making an offer of them to the attention of the *planters.*

It is now nearly 23 years fince I was in the *West-Indies.* Long before that time, down to the prefent, there has not been the leaft difpofition in the *negroes* to *refiftance* and much lefs to *rebellion.* Whilft I was there, fo *docile* were their tempers, fo *paftoral* were their habits, that the *outer* doors of their *mafter's houfe* were never faftened during the *whole* of the *night*—and it muft not be untold, that neither the *overfeer* or any other *white* fervant flept under the fame roof with the mafter. What the practice might now be, *fince* Mr. Wilberforce is beating the *drum* of *fedition* in their ears, I will not take upon me to fay; but this I know, that if the effect *operates* naturally, it will act as it has at *St. Domingo.*

Whether this *fact* which I have ftated will be believed in this land of *freedom,* where *iron plated doors, locks, bolts,* and *chains,* are fometimes *ineffectual* fecurities againft the *iron crow* of the *freebooter,* I will not take upon me to fay—but yet it is a *fact,* and urged by me to prove the *docility* of the negroes, and the *happy* ftate of all their minds.

So far from their not having the power of entering their mafters houfes, if it were their difpofition—they are free enough, at leaft in their perfons, for the exercife of their wills, provided
their

their cruel treatment ever *fuggefted* the *motive* to their hearts :—but inftead of the perpetration of horrid deeds, fuited by the dead of night to minds revengeful for cruelties committed, I fcarcely ever vifited a plantation in the night time, but I heard on one eftate or other, *negroes engaged in dancing to vocal and inftrumental cho-ruffes.*

Whatever alterations I have to offer, are fo *many fubtractions* from the *promifcuous connections* of negroes in their amours. Thefe are acts of *licentioufnefs* incurred by their *doing what they pleafe*, and not a confequence of the reftraining hand of power.

In the prefent ftate, *a young negroe man* will have as *many wives* as his *will* prefcribes, or his *fancy in fucceffion* fuggefts ; and thefe *wives*, as they are called, are fcattered about on *other* eftates often *very remote* from that he belongs to.

So light to a young negroe man is the labour of the day, that he will walk after it for miles to his intended place of reft. The children which he *may* get belong to the. *mafter* of the negroe woman. So that a fine negroe man is wafting the prime of his life in nocturnal perambulations, increafing the family he *cannot* live with, forming attachments he *cannot* fupport, and lef-fening *his own* confequence with his mafter, by not adding to *his value* a family of children.

If

If a master be ever so attentive to the *propagation* of his *negroes*, and if he aims to be as successful in the exercise of his assiduity for obtaining *this point* as in establishing other regulations on his own plantation—yet he *cannot* succeed, because the *practice* of his negroes is a *bar* against it; for by his negroe men cohabiting with the women of *others*, and by his negroe women cohabiting with the men of *others*, the master cannot in that case pursue the system his reason approves, by not having his own *Imperium in Imperio*.

But this is only a preface to my argument.

The negroe woman residing *far* from the man, whom she *sometimes* sees, and is *always* jealous of, in process of time is *sure* to be *deserted*; and then she becomes, as most of them afterwards do, *common* to all. This is the natural effect of inconstancy in every climate and on all constitutions.

Considering that there is on all the islands a *paucity* of *women* in comparison to men (and that is allowed in every calculation) the *chastity* of the *women* becomes a consideration of increased importance. The women who entertain *promiscuous* connections are never *fruitful*.

The cause of barrenness in women of pleasure in this metropolis is truly attributed to *this*. And if the chastity of negroe women be *necessary* to propagation—if it be *necessary* for that end, that a woman should be *constant* to *one* man—that cannot be so well obtained by the negroe man re-

O   siding

fiding on another plantation, and who moſt commonly has not only *one* wife to ſatisfy by his conſtancy, but *many* more.

In every country—to promote propagation, where there is a *paucity* of women, the connection and conſtancy of *one* man to *one* woman are the moſt eſſential means. It has been argued by ſome that the *Turks* have *many* wives, and that they populate in abundance—the faćt is *true*, but the inference, as applicable to theWeſt-Indies, is *wrong*.

In *Turkey* the wars and the plague conſume the *men* more than the *women*, and there is a redundance of women remaining. Inſtead of a *paucity* of *women* there is a *paucity* of *men*, and the *Turk* takes care that his wives ſhall have *no* connećtion with *other* men. This ſyſtem of propagation is certainly ſuited to a paucity of *men*, and therefore the very reverſe to a paucity of *women*. But *promiſcuous* connećtions are deſtrućtive of every ſyſtem.

The comforts of negroes muſt be increaſed by the man cohabiting with the woman; and in point of increaſing *population*, it is moſt certainly the *ſine qua non* of it.

The *negroe wife* ſhould be left to the care of her family and employed in domeſtick purſuits; for if *population* goes on increaſing by this mode, in proceſs of time—the planter will be enabled to make

make that *allowance* which he now allots for the *purchase of negroes.*

When a *negroe youth* is arrived at the age for *marriage* and has made another master's *negroe girl* the object of his choice—and when he has gained the affections of the *girl*—and when they have announced their mutual attachment—the *negroe girl* should be made over to the master of the *youth,* and sent home to him. Such a *marriage* would operate equal to all, as on every plantation there are both men and women.

It is not my part to go minutely into the subject—to follow it up by the adjustments of reciprocal *valuations.* I do not intend to be so dogmatick. I only mean to submit a system, and to be understood as saying, that a *marriage* thus conducted, and, when once performed solemnly adhered to, will promote *propagation.*

Laws against *adultery* should be rigorously enforced. Mr. Wilberforce will not complain if they do press harder there, than in England; where a poor man who gets a bastard child may only be confined till *doomsday,* unless he can purchase out his time, and do away the crime of the flesh by the gold of his pocket.

As this system must have time before it can be put into practice—as there are many prejudices of habit to be weaned—and as those who have already arrived to years of puberty and have formed their connections, cannot be comprised

prifed in it—but as it is only adapted to *boys*
and *girls growing to puberty*, fo muft it have
time to be carried into effect, and time afterwards for the operation of the effect.

During the purfuit of it—the planters muft be
at liberty to *purchafe* what negroes they pleafe ;
for I am confident it will take at leaft fifteen
years before they can be able to fay that the
fyftem will anfwer the end intended : and during
that time—it muft not be forgotten, that the labour of *young women* is loft in the field.

With refpect to the *children*, as long as the
mothers take care of them—they can never be in
better hands : but if any neglect them, or if a
mother dies, there fhould be a publick feminary
for training them in health and inclining their
minds to morality and chaftity.

Raw rum fhould be never fold in common.
Such as know how to ufe it with moderation,
and who require it as a medicine, fhould only
have it. When diftributed to the negroes in
general, it fhould be firft mixed with water ;
and they fhould, if they took it away with them
in their *calebafhes*, be punifhed for felling it to
any other negroe.

It would be very conducive to this plan, if
the negroe *young girls* were particularly attended
to, and if they were trained before they arrived
to maturity for *marriage*, (whilft the fyftem is
new,)

new,) to difcharge the duties they are appointed hereafter to fulfil.

The fact is, that it is the *libidinous practices* of negroes which want *reform*. They are fo amply provided for, and their toil is fo light— they have fo little concern for the provifion of the day—are fo free from the incumbrance of providing for a family—they contribute of them-felves fo little to the wants which create the cares of the *poor* in *other* countries—that their burthen of life is ever light, and their anxiety for their *children* is as fhort as that of a bird whilft its young are fledging.

An eafy accefs to *fpirituous liquors*, and an *unbounded promifcuous connection* of the fexes, are ample caufes for checking population in every climate of the known world.

FINIS.

www.ingramcontent.com/pod-product-compliance
Lightning Source LLC
Chambersburg PA
CBHW030544270326
41927CB00008B/1511